Ladies' Home Journal

100 GREAT

SOUP, STEW &

CHILI RECIPES

LADIES' HOME JOURNAL™ BOOKS
New York/Des Moines

LADIES' HOME JOURNAL™ BOOKS
An Imprint of Meredith® Books
President, Book Group: Joseph J. Ward
Vice President and Editorial Director: Elizabeth P. Rice
Art Director: Ernest Shelton

LADIES' HOME JOURNAL®
Publishing Director and Editor-in-Chief: Myrna Blyth
Food Editor: Jan Turner Hazard
Associate Food Editors: Susan Sarao Westmoreland, Lisa Brainerd

100 GREAT SOUP, STEW & CHILI RECIPES
Project Manager/Editor: Shelli McConnell
Writer/Researcher: Carol Prager
Copy Editor: Jennifer Miller
Associate Art Director: Tom Wegner
Food Stylist: Rick Ellis
Prop Stylist: Bette Blau
Photographer: Corinne Colen Photography
Production Manager: Douglas Johnston
Electronic Production Coordinator: Paula Forest

On the cover: Old-Fashioned Beef Stew, page 74

Meredith Corporation Corporate Officers
Chairman of the Executive Committee: E. T. Meredith III
Chairman of the Board, President and Chief Executive Officer: Jack D. Rehm
Group Presidents: Joseph J. Ward, Books; William T. Kerr, Magazines;
Philip A. Jones, Broadcasting; Allen L. Sabbag, Real Estate
Vice Presidents: Leo R. Armatis, Corporate Relations; Thomas G. Fisher, General Counsel
and Secretary; Larry D. Hartsook, Finance; Michael A. Sell, Treasurer; Kathleen J. Zehr,
Controller and Assistant Secretary

We Care!
All of us at Ladies' Home Journal™ Books are dedicated to providing you with the ideas and
recipe information you need to create wonderful foods. We welcome your comments and
suggestions. Write us at: Ladies' Home Journal™ Books, Cookbook Editorial Department,
RW-240, 1716 Locust St., Des Moines, IA 50309-3023.

If you would like to order additional copies of any of our books, call 1-800-678-2803.

To ensure that Ladies' Home Journal® recipes
meet the highest standards for flavor, nutrition,
appearance and reliability, we test them a
minimum of three times in our own kitchen.
That makes for quality you can count on.

Soups, Stews, and Chilies—The Ultimate Comfort Foods

What is it about a bowl of soup that makes us feel good? Maybe it's the vision of the soup kettle simmering on the back of your grandmother's stove. Or, maybe it's the memory of a bowl of chicken noodle soup served to you when you stayed home from school with a cold. The fact is that a steaming bowl of soup, stew, or chili makes us feel good, and savoring each delicious spoonful makes us feel even better. Most soups, stews, and chilis are a cinch to make because they cook in one pot. And as they cook, the flavors of all the ingredients meld together for a finished dish that is more than a sum of its parts. So, whether you choose a humble soup, an elegant stew, or a rough-and-tumble chili, you'll find the cooking easy.

Contents

Simply Splendid Starters

Light and refreshing, these hot and cold soups offer perfect beginnings to delicious meals.

Hearty Main Course Soups

Flavorful entrées guaranteed to stick to the ribs and warm the tummy.

Simply for Comfort Stews

Richly satisfying stews that are so easy to make.

Festive Stews

Company pleasing bowlfuls perfect for carefree entertaining.

Wild About Chili

A round-up of firey bowls of red along with milder selections.

Index

SIMPLY SPLENDID

STARTERS

Whether you're eating alone or with friends, this perfect blend of light refreshing soups will get your next meal off to just the right start. Warm up our emerald green Elegant Watercress Soup, Satiny Butternut Squash Soup sweetened with apples, or Italian White Bean and Garlic Soup mellowed with the slow-roasted flavor of garlic and onions. Also featured are "souper" cool Classic Gazpacho served with Garlic Croutons and Chilled Carrot Soup with Tarragon, both perfect for do-ahead summertime entertaining.

PEACHY CANTALOUPE SOUP

For a touch of elegance and pure refreshment when dining on a hot summer's day, nothing beats fruit soup as a first course.

▼ *Low-fat*
▽ *Low-calorie*
   Prep time: 15 minutes plus chilling
○ *Degree of difficulty: easy*

  1 **medium ripe cantaloupe, peeled, seeded, and cut into chunks**
  1 **medium ripe peach, peeled, seeded, and cut into chunks**
  ½ **cup white wine**
  ¼ **cup fresh orange juice**
  1 **tablespoon granulated sugar**
 1½ **cups buttermilk**
     Sliced fresh peaches

1 Place cantaloupe, peach, wine, orange juice, and sugar in a food processor or blender. Process or blend until almost smooth. Add buttermilk and process until well blended.

2 Transfer soup mixture to a large bowl. Cover and refrigerate until cold and flavors are blended, 2 hours or overnight. Spoon soup into chilled bowls and garnish each with sliced peaches. Makes 6 servings.

PER SERVING		DAILY GOAL
Calories	91	2,000 (F), 2,500 (M)
Total Fat	1 g	60 g or less (F), 70 g or less (M)
Saturated fat	0 g	20 g or less (F), 23 g or less (M)
Cholesterol	2 mg	300 mg or less
Sodium	73 mg	2,400 mg or less
Carbohydrates	16 g	250 g or more
Protein	3 g	55 g to 90 g

NOTES

MINTED PEA SOUP

Lettuce gives this delicate soup a lovely smooth texture; use either iceberg or romaine lettuce.

▽ *Low-calorie*
 Prep time: 10 minutes
 Cooking time: 20 minutes
○ *Degree of difficulty: easy*

¼ cup butter *or* margarine
1 package (10 ounces) frozen baby peas
2 cups coarsely shredded iceberg *or* Romaine lettuce
1 green onion, coarsely chopped
1 can (13¾ *or* 14½ ounces) chicken broth plus enough water to equal 3 cups *or* 3 cups Rich Chicken Stock (recipe, page 29)
3 tablespoons coarsely chopped fresh mint leaves
2 teaspoons fresh lemon juice
⅛ teaspoon salt
⅛ teaspoon white pepper
 Sour cream, for garnish

1 Melt the butter or margarine in a medium saucepan over medium heat. Add peas, lettuce, and onion and cook, stirring occasionally, until vegetables are very tender, 15 minutes. Add the chicken broth and simmer 5 minutes. Remove from heat and stir in the mint, lemon juice, salt, and pepper.

2 Puree soup in a blender in small batches and return each batch to the saucepan. Spoon soup into warm bowls and garnish each with sour cream. Makes 6 servings.

PER SERVING WITHOUT SOUR CREAM

		DAILY GOAL
Calories	110	2,000 (F), 2,500 (M)
Total Fat	9 g	60 g or less (F), 70 g or less (M)
Saturated fat	5 g	20 g or less (F), 23 g or less (M)
Cholesterol	21 mg	300 mg or less
Sodium	531 mg	2,400 mg or less
Carbohydrates	7 g	250 g or more
Protein	3 g	55 g to 90 g

CHILLED CARROT SOUP WITH TARRAGON

This cold soup couldn't be simpler or more elegant for summer entertaining. If tarragon is not to your taste, try other fresh herbs, such as dill or chervil. *Also pictured on page 6.*

▽ *Low-calorie*
Prep time: 25 minutes plus chilling
Cooking time: 20 to 30 minutes
○ *Degree of difficulty: easy*

1 **tablespoon vegetable oil**
1½ **cups chopped onions**
1 **pound peeled carrots, chopped (2½ cups)**
1 **can (13¾ or 14½ ounces) chicken broth or 1¾ cups Rich Chicken Stock (recipe, page 29)**
3½ **cups water**
1 **slice lemon**
1 **teaspoon salt**
¼ **teaspoon freshly ground pepper Pinch thyme**
1 **tablespoon chopped fresh tarragon**
¼ **teaspoon grated lemon peel**

1 **container (8 ounces) plain yogurt Fresh tarragon sprigs, for garnish**

1 Heat oil in a saucepan over medium heat. Add onions and cook, stirring occasionally, until tender, 5 minutes. Add carrots, chicken broth, water, lemon, salt, pepper, and thyme; bring to a boil. Reduce heat and simmer uncovered until carrots are very tender, 20 to 30 minutes. Remove lemon slice.

2 Puree soup in a blender in small batches and transfer each batch to a large bowl. Cool to room temperature. Cover and refrigerate until completely cold, 4 hours or overnight. (Can be made ahead. Cover and refrigerate up to 2 days.)

3 Just before serving, stir in tarragon and season to taste with salt and pepper. Stir lemon peel into yogurt. Spoon soup into chilled bowls and top each with 2 tablespoons yogurt and a tarragon sprig. Makes 6 servings.

PER SERVING		DAILY GOAL
Calories	105	2,000 (F), 2,500 (M)
Total Fat	4 g	60 g or less (F), 70 g or less (M)
Saturated fat	1 g	20 g or less (F), 23 g or less (M)
Cholesterol	2 mg	300 mg or less
Sodium	762 mg	2,400 mg or less
Carbohydrates	15 g	250 g or more
Protein	4 g	55 g to 90 g

NOTES

CAULIFLOWER SOUP WITH FRAGRANT CROUTONS

The homemade curried croutons add an unexpected, spicy flavor to this easy soup.

▽ *Low-calorie*
Prep time: 20 minutes
Cooking time: 30 minutes
○ *Degree of difficulty: easy*

6 **tablespoons butter** *or* **margarine**
3 **cups chopped onions**
3 **tablespoons all-purpose flour**
6 **cups canned chicken broth** *or* **Rich Chicken Stock (recipe, page 29)**
2 **medium heads (5 pounds) cauliflower, cut into florets**
1½ **cups half-and-half cream**
¾ **teaspoon salt**
⅛ **teaspoon white pepper**

Curry Croutons
6 **tablespoons butter** *or* **margarine, melted**
1 **tablespoon curry powder**
4 **cups ½-inch bread cubes (about 10 slices firm white bread)**

1 Melt butter in a large saucepan over medium-high heat. Add onions, cover and cook until tender, 5 minutes. Stir in flour and cook, stirring, 1 minute. Stir in chicken broth, then cauliflower; bring to a boil. Reduce heat and simmer 20 minutes or until cauliflower is fork-tender.

2 Puree soup in a blender or food processor in small batches and return each batch to the saucepan. Stir in cream, salt, and pepper. (Can be made ahead. Cool to room temperature. Cover and refrigerate up to 2 days. Reheat in a large saucepan over medium-high heat until hot, about 15 minutes.) Cook 2 minutes longer or until just heated through. Spoon soup into warm bowls and sprinkle each with Curry Croutons. Makes 16 servings.

Curry Croutons: Preheat oven to 350°F. Combine butter and curry powder in a medium bowl; set aside. Arrange bread cubes in a jelly-roll pan. Bake 15 to 20 minutes, stirring halfway through, until bread is dry and lightly toasted. Immediately toss with butter mixture. Return to pan and cool completely. (Can be made ahead. Cover and store at room temperature up to 2 days.)

PER SERVING WITH CROUTONS		DAILY GOAL
Calories	191	2,000 (F), 2,500 (M)
Total Fat	13 g	60 g or less (F), 70 g or less (M)
Saturated fat	7 g	20 g or less (F), 23 g or less (M)
Cholesterol	32 mg	300 mg or less
Sodium	728 mg	2,400 mg or less
Carbohydrates	16 g	250 g or more
Protein	4 g	55 g to 90 g

NOTES

CURRIED BROCCOLI SOUP

Fresh broccoli soup has always been one of our most requested recipes. In this version we've added potato for creaminess without additional fat.

▼ *Low-fat*
▽ *Low-calorie*
   Prep time: 10 minutes
   Cooking time: 30 minutes
○ *Degree of difficulty: easy*

2 **teaspoons olive oil**
1 **cup chopped onions**
2 **teaspoons minced garlic**
1 **teaspoon curry powder**
2 **cans (13¾ *or* 14½ ounces each) low-sodium chicken broth plus enough water to equal 3 cups *or* 3 cups Rich Chicken Stock (recipe, page 29)**
4 **cups chopped broccoli**
1 **cup peeled, diced potato**
   Salt
   Plain nonfat *or* low-fat yogurt

1 Heat oil in a large saucepan over medium heat. Add onions, garlic, and curry powder; cover and cook 3 minutes. Stir in chicken broth, broccoli, and potato. Bring to a boil. Cover and simmer until vegetables are tender, 25 minutes.

2 Puree soup in a blender in small batches and return each batch to the saucepan. Season with salt to taste. Spoon soup into warm bowls and top each with 1 tablespoon yogurt. Makes 5 servings.

PER SERVING		DAILY GOAL
Calories	104	2,000 (F), 2,500 (M)
Total Fat	3 g	60 g or less (F), 70 g or less (M)
Saturated fat	1 g	20 g or less (F), 23 g or less (M)
Cholesterol	0 mg	300 mg or less
Sodium	71 mg	2,400 mg or less
Carbohydrates	15 g	250 g or more
Protein	6 g	55 g to 90 g

NOTES

13

CHILLED DILL-SQUASH SOUP

Here's the perfect way to take advantage of a bumper crop of golden summer squash.

▽   *Low-calorie*
    Prep time: 20 minutes plus chilling
    Cooking time: 40 minutes
○   *Degree of difficulty: easy*

2 **tablespoons vegetable oil**
½ **cup chopped onion**
⅓ **cup chopped celery**
⅓ **cup chopped peeled carrot**
1½ **pounds yellow summer squash, cut into ½-inch cubes**
¾ **cup peeled, diced potato**
2½ **cups water**
1 **can (13¾ or 14½ ounces) chicken broth or 1¾ cups Rich Chicken Stock (recipe, page 29)**
1 **can (13¾ or 14½ ounces) beef broth or 1¾ cups Hearty Beef Stock (recipe, page 30)**
2 **tablespoons chopped fresh dill**
½ **cup heavy or whipping cream**

½ **teaspoon salt**
¼ **teaspoon freshly ground pepper**
   Chopped fresh dill, for garnish

1 Heat oil in a large saucepan over medium heat. Add onion, celery, and carrot; cook until tender, 4 minutes. Add squash; cover and cook 5 minutes. Stir in potato, water, and chicken and beef broths. Bring to a boil, then reduce heat and simmer until potato is tender, 30 minutes.

2 Puree soup in a blender in small batches and transfer each batch to a large bowl. Add dill, cream, salt, and pepper. Cover and refrigerate until chilled, at least 2 hours. Spoon soup into chilled cups and garnish each with dill. Makes 8 servings.

PER SERVING		DAILY GOAL
Calories	130	2,000 (F), 2,500 (M)
Total Fat	10 g	60 g or less (F), 70 g or less (M)
Saturated fat	4 g	20 g or less (F), 23 g or less (M)
Cholesterol	20 mg	300 mg or less
Sodium	639 mg	2,400 mg or less
Carbohydrates	8 g	250 g or more
Protein	2 g	55 g to 90 g

NOTES

SATINY BUTTERNUT SQUASH SOUP

The flavors in this autumn squash soup are very subtle—the apple adds sweetness and the curry powder provides a touch of spice.

▽ *Low-calorie*
Prep time: 20 minutes
Cooking time: 30 minutes
○ *Degree of difficulty: easy*

2 tablespoons butter *or* margarine
1 medium onion, chopped
1 carrot, peeled and chopped
1 teaspoon curry powder
3 cans (13¾ *or* 14½ ounces each) chicken broth *or* 5¼ cups Rich Chicken Stock (recipe, page 29)
2 large butternut squash (about 3 pounds), peeled, seeded, and coarsely chopped
2 baking apples, peeled, cored, and coarsely chopped
¼ teaspoon freshly ground pepper
Plain low-fat yogurt and apple slices, for garnish

1 Melt butter in a large saucepan over medium heat. Add onion, carrot, and curry powder; cook until onion is softened, 5 minutes. Add chicken broth, squash, apples, and pepper. Simmer until vegetables are tender, 12 minutes.

2 Puree soup in a blender in small batches and return each batch to the saucepan. (Can be made ahead. Transfer soup to a large bowl and cool to room temperature. Cover and refrigerate up to 2 days. Reheat in a saucepan 15 minutes.) Spoon soup into warm bowls and garnish each with a dollop of yogurt and apple slices. Makes 10 servings.

PER SERVING WITHOUT GARNISHES

		DAILY GOAL
Calories	117	2,000 (F), 2,500 (M)
Total Fat	4 g	60 g or less (F), 70 g or less (M)
Saturated fat	1 g	20 g or less (F), 23 g or less (M)
Cholesterol	6 mg	300 mg or less
Sodium	645 mg	2,400 mg or less
Carbohydrates	21 g	250 g or more
Protein	2 g	55 g to 90 g

NOTES

15

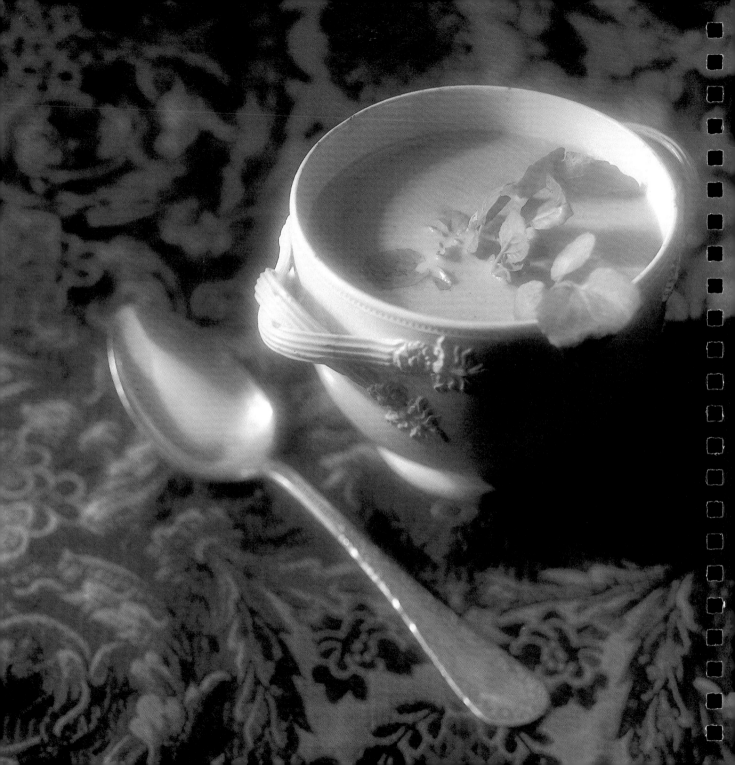

ELEGANT WATERCRESS SOUP

By simply cutting all the ingredients in half, this emerald green soup can be served to a smaller gathering of friends.

▽ *Low-calorie*
Prep time: 25 minutes
Cooking time: 40 minutes
○ *Degree of difficulty: easy*

¼ cup butter *or* margarine
2 cups chopped leeks, white
  part only
1 cup chopped onions
1 teaspoon minced garlic
8 cups packed watercress (3 large
  bunches), tough ends trimmed
1 head Romaine lettuce, shredded
  (about 7 cups)
½ cup all-purpose flour
4 cans (13¾ *or* 14½ ounces each)
  chicken broth *or* 7 cups Rich
  Chicken Stock (recipe, page 29)
4 cups water
1½ teaspoons salt
⅛ teaspoon white pepper
2 cups half-and-half cream

2 tablespoons fresh lemon juice
  Watercress sprigs, for garnish

1 Melt butter in a large Dutch oven over medium heat. Add leeks and onions; cook, stirring occasionally, until tender, about 5 minutes. Stir in garlic, then watercress and Romaine. Cook, stirring occasionally, until lettuces are wilted, about 10 minutes. Add the flour and cook, stirring constantly, 2 minutes. Add the chicken broth, water, salt, and pepper; bring to a boil, stirring constantly. Reduce heat and simmer uncovered 20 minutes.

2 Puree soup in a blender in small batches. (Can be made ahead. Transfer to a large bowl and cool completely. Cover and refrigerate up to 24 hours.) Return to Dutch oven and heat to a simmer. Stir in cream and lemon juice and continue to cook until just heated through *(do not boil)*. Immediately spoon soup into bowls and garnish each with a watercress sprig. Makes 12 servings.

PER SERVING		DAILY GOAL
Calories	150	2,000 (F), 2,500 (M)
Total Fat	10 g	60 g or less (F), 70 g or less (M)
Saturated fat	5 g	20 g or less (F), 23 g or less (M)
Cholesterol	25 mg	300 mg or less
Sodium	1,028 mg	2,400 mg or less
Carbohydrates	11g	250 g or more
Protein	4 g	55 g to 90 g

NOTES

17

CHILLED RED PEPPER SOUP

This lovely soup with a fresh basil accent can be prepared with any color of sweet bell pepper.

▽ *Low-calorie*
   Prep time: 15 minutes plus chilling
   Cooking time: 35 minutes
○ *Degree of difficulty: easy*

3 **tablespoons olive oil**
3 **cups chopped red peppers**
2 **cups chopped onions**
½ **teaspoon thyme**
1 **tablespoon minced garlic**
⅛ **teaspoon ground red pepper**
2 **cans (13¾ *or* 14½ ounces each)**
   chicken broth *or* 3½ cups Rich
   Chicken Stock (recipe, page 29)
½ **teaspoon salt**
2 **cups buttermilk**
¼ **cup shredded fresh basil**

1 Heat oil in a large saucepan over medium-high heat. Add peppers, onions, and thyme; cook, stirring occasionally, until vegetables have softened, 15 minutes. Add garlic and ground pepper; cook 30 seconds. Stir in the chicken broth and salt; bring to a boil. Reduce heat and simmer covered 20 minutes.

2 Puree soup in a blender or food processor in small batches and return each batch to the saucepan. Strain soup through a sieve into a large bowl. Refrigerate until cold, 4 hours. Whisk in buttermilk. (Can be made ahead. Cover and refrigerate up to 2 days.) Spoon soup into chilled bowls and sprinkle each with basil. Makes 8 servings.

PER SERVING		DAILY GOAL
Calories	113	2,000 (F), 2,500 (M)
Total Fat	7 g	60 g or less (F), 70 g or less (M)
Saturated fat	1 g	20 g or less (F), 23 g or less (M)
Cholesterol	2 mg	300 mg or less
Sodium	715 mg	2,400 mg or less
Carbohydrates	10 g	250 g or more
Protein	4 g	55 g to 90 g

NOTES

FRESH CORN, ZUCCHINI, AND TOMATO CHOWDER

When the autumn nights turn chilly, what could be more warming than this harvest vegetable soup?

▽ *Low-calorie*
   Prep time: 15 minutes
   Cooking time: 20 minutes
○ *Degree of difficulty: easy*

1 **tablespoon butter** *or* **margarine**
1 **cup chopped onions**
1 **teaspoon minced garlic**
3 **cups fresh corn kernels, divided (6 ears)**
1 **can (13¾** *or* **14½ ounces) chicken broth** *or* **1¾ cups Rich Chicken Stock (recipe, page 29)**
1 **tomato, seeded and diced**
1 **cup diced zucchini**
¼ **cup heavy** *or* **whipping cream**
2 **tablespoons julienned fresh basil**
2 **tablespoons minced fresh chives**
   Salt and freshly ground pepper

1 Melt butter in a large saucepan over medium heat. Add the onions and garlic; cover and cook until onions are tender, 3 minutes. Stir in 2 cups of the corn and chicken broth; bring to a boil. Reduce heat and simmer covered 5 minutes.

2 Puree soup in a blender in small batches and return each batch to the saucepan. Add remaining 1 cup corn, tomato, and zucchini. Cover and simmer 5 minutes. Remove from heat and stir in cream, basil, and chives. Season with salt and pepper to taste. Spoon soup into warm bowls. Makes 4 servings.

PER SERVING		DAILY GOAL
Calories	220	2,000 (F), 2,500 (M)
Total Fat	11 g	60 g or less (F), 70 g or less (M)
Saturated fat	5 g	20 g or less (F), 23 g or less (M)
Cholesterol	28 mg	300 mg or less
Sodium	570 mg	2,400 mg or less
Carbohydrates	29 g	250 g or more
Protein	6 g	55 g to 90 g

NOTES

VELVET CORN-CILANTRO SOUP

For a hint of extra flavor, add a tablespoon of dry sherry to this golden soup just before serving.

▽   *Low-calorie*
    Prep time: 10 minutes
    Cooking time: 10 minutes
○   *Degree of difficulty: easy*

1   **tablespoon vegetable oil**
¼   **cup chopped green onions**
2   **cans (13¾ *or* 14½ ounces each) chicken broth *or* 3½ cups Rich Chicken Stock (recipe, page 29)**
1   **can (17 ounces) creamed corn**
1   **tablespoon cornstarch**
2   **tablespoons water**
2   **large egg whites, slightly beaten**
2   **tablespoons chopped fresh cilantro**
¼   **teaspoon freshly ground pepper**
¼   **cup finely chopped baked ham**

1 Heat oil in a medium saucepan over medium-high heat. Add green onions and cook 1 minute. Carefully add the chicken broth and creamed corn, then cover and bring to a simmer.

2 Meanwhile, combine cornstarch and water in a cup until smooth. Stir into soup and simmer 1 minute. Remove from heat. Slowly stir in beaten egg whites, then add cilantro and pepper. Immediately spoon soup into bowls and top each with chopped ham. Makes 4 servings.

PER SERVING		DAILY GOAL
Calories	181	2,000 (F), 2,500 (M)
Total Fat	7 g	60 g or less (F), 70 g or less (M)
Saturated fat	1 g	20 g or less (F), 23 g or less (M)
Cholesterol	5 mg	300 mg or less
Sodium	1,527 mg	2,400 mg or less
Carbohydrates	25 g	250 g or more
Protein	7 g	55 g to 90 g

NOTES

AUSTRIAN CREAMED POTATO SOUP

Here's an unusual potato soup, warm and creamy with spices, white wine, and a touch of caraway.

▽ *Low-calorie*
Prep time: 20 minutes
Cooking time: 30 minutes
○ *Degree of difficulty: easy*

3 **cans (13¾ *or* 14½ ounces each) beef broth *or* 5¼ cups Hearty Beef Stock (recipe, page 30)**
2 **pounds peeled, cubed potatoes (5 cups)**
¾ **teaspoon caraway seeds, crushed**
¼ **teaspoon marjoram, crushed**
¼ **teaspoon salt**
⅛ **teaspoon freshly ground pepper**
⅛ **teaspoon ginger**
½ **cup white wine**
1 **tablespoon all-purpose flour**
¾ **cup sour cream**
¾ **cup heavy *or* whipping cream**
Chopped fresh parsley, for garnish

1 Combine beef broth, potatoes, caraway, marjoram, salt, pepper, and ginger in a large saucepan. Bring to a boil over medium-high heat. Reduce heat to medium; cover and cook until potatoes are fork-tender, 15 minutes. Add wine and cook 5 minutes.

2 Meanwhile, whisk flour and sour cream in a small bowl until smooth. Stir in ½ cup hot broth. Gradually add sour cream mixture to soup, stirring constantly. Cook 5 minutes, stirring occasionally. Add heavy cream and cook until just heated through, 2 minutes more. Spoon soup into warm bowls and garnish each with chopped parsley. Makes 9 servings.

PER SERVING		DAILY GOAL
Calories	214	2,000 (F), 2,500 (M)
Total Fat	12 g	60 g or less (F), 70 g or less (M)
Saturated fat	7 g	20 g or less (F), 23 g or less (M)
Cholesterol	36 mg	300 mg or less
Sodium	702 mg	2,400 mg or less
Carbohydrates	21 g	250 g or more
Protein	4 g	55 g to 90 g

NOTES

VEGETABLE PATCH SOUP

Here's a batch of soup made with fresh fixin's from the garden.

▼ *Low-fat*
▽ *Low-calorie*
  Prep time: 15 minutes
  Cooking time: 45 minutes
○ *Degree of difficulty: easy*

1 tablespoon vegetable oil
1¼ pounds yams *or* butternut squash, peeled and cut into ½-inch cubes
3 carrots, peeled and cut into ½-inch chunks (1½ cups)
1½ cups diced onions
8 ounces fresh mushrooms, sliced
2 garlic cloves, peeled and halved
1 teaspoon salt *or* to taste
1 teaspoon Italian seasoning
½ teaspoon freshly ground pepper
2 cans (13¾ *or* 14½ ounces each) chicken broth *or* 3½ cups Rich Chicken Stock (recipe, page 29) *or* Classic Vegetable Stock (recipe, page 31)
5 cups water
¾ cup orzo *or* other small pasta
1 package (10 ounces) frozen peas
1 package (10 ounces) frozen leaf spinach

1 Heat oil in a large Dutch oven over medium-high heat. Add yams or squash, carrots, onions, mushrooms, garlic, salt, Italian seasoning, and pepper. Cook, stirring, until vegetables begin to brown, 10 minutes.

2 Add broth and water; bring to a boil. Reduce heat to low and cover and simmer 20 minutes. Return to a boil over medium-high heat. Stir in orzo and cook uncovered 5 minutes. Stir in peas and spinach and return to a boil. Cook until orzo is tender, 5 minutes more. Makes 16 servings.

PER SERVING		DAILY GOAL
Calories	115	2,000 (F), 2,500 (M)
Total Fat	2 g	60 g or less (F), 70 g or less (M)
Saturated fat	0 g	20 g or less (F), 23 g or less (M)
Cholesterol	0 mg	300 mg or less
Sodium	308 mg	2,400 mg or less
Carbohydrates	22 g	250 g or more
Protein	4 g	55 g to 90 g

SHE-CRAB SOUP

Crab roe gives this delicate soup from the South its name and wonderfully rich flavor.

▽ *Low-calorie*
  Prep time: 20 minutes
  Cooking time: 15 minutes
○ *Degree of difficulty: easy*

2 **tablespoons butter *or* margarine, divided**
½ **cup chopped onion**
⅛ **teaspoon mace**
2 **tablespoons all-purpose flour**
1 **bottle (8 ounces) clam juice**
2 **cups milk**
8 **ounces flaked crabmeat**
½ **teaspoon salt**
¼ **teaspoon freshly ground pepper**
  Crab roe* *or* 1 hard-cooked egg yolk, sieved
½ **teaspoon fresh lemon juice**
4 **tablespoons dry sherry**
  Paprika
  Chopped fresh parsley

1 Melt 1 tablespoon of the butter in a large saucepan over medium heat. Add onion and mace; cook until onion is tender, about 5 minutes. Add flour and cook, stirring, 1 minute. Whisk in clam juice, then milk. Add crabmeat, salt, and pepper. Cook, stirring occasionally, 10 to 15 minutes.

2 Meanwhile, melt remaining 1 tablespoon butter in a small skillet over medium heat. Add roe and cook, stirring, 1 minute. Remove from heat and stir in lemon juice. Stir roe or egg yolk, if using, into soup.

3 Pour 1 tablespoon of the sherry in the bottom of each of 4 warm soup bowls. Add soup and sprinkle with paprika and chopped parsley. Makes 4 servings.

*Crab roe: In a large stockpot, bring to boil enough salted water to cover 2 to 3 female crabs. Plunge crabs in head first. Cover and return to a boil. Simmer 12 to 15 minutes, until crabs turn red. Drain. Pick out meat and roe and reserve for soup.

PER SERVING		DAILY GOAL
Calories	245	2,000 (F), 2,500 (M)
Total Fat	12 g	60 g or less (F), 70 g or less (M)
Saturated fat	7 g	20 g or less (F), 23 g or less (M)
Cholesterol	142 mg	300 mg or less
Sodium	683 mg	2,400 mg or less
Carbohydrates	12 g	250 g or more
Protein	17 g	55 g to 90 g

SEAFOOD GAZPACHO

Three ingredients make this version of gazpacho special: spicy vegetable juice, fresh shellfish, and chopped cilantro.

▽ *Low-calorie*
  Total prep time: 40 minutes plus chilling
○ *Degree of difficulty: easy*

1 **cup diced onions**
2 **cucumbers, peeled, seeded, and diced (1 cup)**
1 **red pepper, diced (½ cup)**
1 **green pepper, diced (½ cup)**
1 **can (35 ounces) Italian plum tomatoes, drained and finely diced (1 cup)**
1 **teaspoon minced garlic**
1 **cup tomato juice**
2 **green onions, thinly sliced**

4½ cups spicy vegetable juice
¼ cup olive oil
2 tablespoons red wine vinegar
1½ teaspoons salt
¾ teaspoon freshly ground pepper
¼ teaspoon red pepper sauce
8 ounces shrimp, peeled, deveined, cooked, and coarsely chopped
8 ounces sea scallops, cooked and sliced
¼ cup chopped fresh cilantro

1 Combine onions, cucumbers, red pepper, green pepper, tomatoes, garlic, and tomato juice in a food processor. Puree until smooth and transfer to a large bowl. Stir in green onions, spicy vegetable juice, oil, vinegar, salt, ground pepper, red pepper sauce, shrimp, and scallops.

2 Cover and refrigerate 2 hours or overnight. Just before serving, stir in cilantro. Makes 8 servings.

PER SERVING		DAILY GOAL
Calories	190	2,000 (F), 2,500 (M)
Total Fat	8 g	60 g or less (F), 70 g or less (M)
Saturated fat	1 g	20 g or less (F), 23 g or less (M)
Cholesterol	45 mg	300 mg or less
Sodium	1,239 mg	2,400 mg or less
Carbohydrates	19 g	250 g or more
Protein	13 g	55 g to 90 g

SMART SEAFOOD SHOPPING: HOW TO BUY FISH

1 Follow your nose. Remember, fish should always smell clean, not fishy.

2 Take a good look. When it comes to the appearance of seafood, you should always check its vital signs.

• When purchasing fish in its whole state, the flesh should always spring back when gently pressed. The scales should be tightly attached to the skin and appear shiny. The eyes should be bulging and clear. The gills should appear red or clear pink.

• Fish fillets should be evenly colored with no bruises or browning around the edges. The meat shouldn't be falling from the bone.

• Clams, oysters, and mussels should be tightly closed and feel heavy for their size. If the shells are open, tap them and they should close immediately. If they don't close they aren't fresh.

• Shucked oysters should be packed in liquid that's clear, not milky.

• Uncooked shrimp are pale pink to shimmery grey and should look firm and plump.

• Fresh scallops should be pinkish, white or pale yellow and give off a clear liquid. They should also feel firm.

• Lobster and crab must be purchased live (unless they are flash-frozen). They should be ready to snap their claws at the slightest provocation.

3 Keep fresh fish cold. Place fish in a large shallow dish or roasting pan in one layer and cover with crushed ice, then cover pan with plastic wrap. Pour off water and replenish ice when needed. If you know the fish arrived at the market the day it was purchased, it will keep refrigerated up to 2 days.

CLASSIC GAZPACHO

No other soup shows off the glory of peak summer vegetables better than this no-cook classic. Include a crunchy batch of homemade garlic croutons along with the traditional vegetable garnishes.

▽ *Low-calorie*
   Total prep time: 30 minutes plus chilling
○ *Degree of difficulty: easy*

3   **pounds very ripe tomatoes, peeled, seeded, and chopped (8 cups)**
1   **cucumber, peeled, seeded, and chopped**
½   **green pepper, chopped**
½   **red pepper, chopped**
½   **yellow pepper, chopped**
3   **tablespoons red wine vinegar**
2   **tablespoons extra-virgin olive oil**
2   **tablespoons chopped red onion**
1   **teaspoon salt**
½   **teaspoon freshly ground pepper**
1   **teaspoon minced garlic**

Garnishes
1   **very ripe tomato, peeled, seeded, and diced**
1   **cucumber, peeled, seeded, and diced**
½   **green pepper, diced**
½   **red pepper, diced**
½   **yellow pepper, diced**
¼   **cup minced red onion**
    Garlic Croutons (recipe, page 62)

1 Combine tomatoes, cucumber, peppers, vinegar, oil, red onion, salt, and pepper in a large bowl. Puree soup in a blender in small batches and transfer each batch to another bowl. Stir in garlic. Cover and refrigerate at least 3 hours or overnight. Spoon soup into chilled bowls and serve garnishes separately. Makes 8 servings.

PER SERVING
WITHOUT CROUTONS | DAILY GOAL
--- | --- | ---
Calories | 130 | 2,000 (F), 2,500 (M)
Total Fat | 6 g | 60 g or less (F), 70 g or less (M)
Saturated fat | 1 g | 20 g or less (F), 23 g or less (M)
Cholesterol | 0 mg | 300 mg or less
Sodium | 347 mg | 2,400 mg or less
Carbohydrates | 18 g | 250 g or more
Protein | 3 g | 55 g to 90 g

ITALIAN WHITE BEAN AND GARLIC SOUP

Slowly cooking the garlic until it's golden brings out its sweet, mellow flavor.

Prep time: 20 minutes
Cooking time: 30 minutes
○ *Degree of difficulty: easy*

2 **tablespoons olive oil**
12 **large cloves garlic, mashed**
1 **can (13¾ or 14½ ounces) chicken broth or 1¾ cups Rich Chicken Stock (recipe, page 29)**
1 **cup water**
1 **can (19 ounces) cannellini beans, drained and rinsed**
½ **teaspoon salt**
½ **teaspoon freshly ground pepper**
1 **bay leaf**
¼ **cup heavy or whipping cream**
8 **slices French or Italian bread**
1 **tablespoon freshly grated Parmesan cheese**

1 Heat oil in a medium saucepan over medium-low heat. Add garlic and cook until soft and golden, 10 minutes.

2 Meanwhile, combine chicken broth, water, beans, salt, pepper, and bay leaf in another saucepan. Bring to a boil. Stir into garlic mixture and simmer 15 minutes. Remove bay leaf. Puree soup in a blender in small batches and return each batch to the saucepan. Stir in cream and keep warm.

3 Preheat broiler. Arrange bread on a cookie sheet and toast both sides lightly. Sprinkle tops with Parmesan and broil 3 minutes, or until cheese is golden and bubbly. Spoon soup into warm bowls and top each with 2 slices of toast. Makes 4 servings.

PER SERVING		DAILY GOAL
Calories	384	2,000 (F), 2,500 (M)
Total Fat	16 g	60 g or less (F), 70 g or less (M)
Saturated fat	5 g	20 g or less (F), 23 g or less (M)
Cholesterol	22 mg	300 mg or less
Sodium	1,293 mg	2,400 mg or less
Carbohydrates	46 g	250 g or more
Protein	14 g	55 g to 90 g

NOTES

28

RICH CHICKEN STOCK

Be sure to thoroughly wash the chicken before adding it to the stockpot. You may also substitute a selection of backs, wings, and necks for the whole chicken.

▽ *Low-calorie*
  Prep time: 5 minutes
  Cooking time: 3½ hours
○ *Degree of difficulty: easy*

1 **whole chicken (4 pounds)**
3 **carrots, peeled and cut into 1-inch pieces**
2 **ribs celery, cut into 1-inch pieces**
2 **large onions, chopped**
3 **garlic cloves, crushed**
4 **sprigs fresh parsley**
1 **sprig fresh thyme *or* ½ teaspoon dried**
1 **bay leaf**
2 **teaspoons salt**
8 **whole peppercorns**
14 **cups water**

1 Combine chicken, carrots, celery, onions, garlic, parsley, thyme, bay leaf, salt, peppercorns, and water in a large Dutch oven; bring to a boil over medium-high heat. Reduce heat and simmer uncovered 2½ hours, occasionally skimming foam and fat from surface. Remove from heat. Strain through a fine sieve into a large bowl; discard solids. Reserve chicken for another use.

2 Return broth to Dutch oven or stockpot; bring to a boil. Reduce heat and simmer uncovered until reduced by half, 30 minutes. Skim off fat. (Can be made ahead. Cool. Transfer to a freezer container, cover and freeze up to 1 month.) Makes 6 cups.

PER 1 CUP		DAILY GOAL
Calories	69	2,000 (F), 2,500 (M)
Total Fat	3 g	60 g or less (F), 70 g or less (M)
Saturated fat	1 g	20 g or less (F), 23 g or less (M)
Cholesterol	0 mg	300 mg or less
Sodium	842 mg	2,400 mg or less
Carbohydrates	5 g	250 g or more
Protein	5 g	55 g to 90 g

TAKING STOCK: A WONDERFUL BEGINNING TO THE BEST TASTING SOUPS, STEWS, AND CHILIES

It takes less than 15 minutes to fix our best homemade chicken, beef, and vegetable stocks. Slowly simmered and richly flavored, these stocks can all be prepared in advance and frozen. Ready at a moment's notice, any of these beautiful broths will make your next soup, stew, or chili have that delicious from-scratch flavor we all love.

HEARTY BEEF STOCK

Trim the excess fat from the beef bones before you begin the slow simmer.

▼ *Low-fat*
▽ *Low-calorie*
  Prep time: 5 minutes
  Cooking time: 3½ hours
○ *Degree of difficulty: easy*

4½ **pounds meaty beef shank bones**
3 **carrots, peeled and cut into 1-inch pieces**
2 **ribs celery, cut into 1-inch pieces**
2 **large onions, chopped**
3 **garlic cloves, crushed**
4 **sprigs fresh parsley**
1 **sprig fresh thyme *or* ½ teaspoon dried**
1 **bay leaf**
2 **teaspoons salt**
8 **whole peppercorns**
14 **cups water**

1 Combine bones, carrots, celery, onions, garlic, parsley, thyme, bay leaf, salt, peppercorns, and water in a large Dutch oven or stockpot; bring to a boil over medium-high heat. Reduce heat and simmer uncovered 2½ hours, occasionally skimming foam and fat from surface. Remove from heat. Strain through a fine sieve into a large bowl; discard solids.

2 Return broth to Dutch oven; bring to a boil. Reduce heat and simmer uncovered until reduced by half, 30 minutes. Skim off fat. (Can be made ahead. Cool. Transfer to a freezer container, cover and freeze up to 1 month.) Makes 6 cups.

PER 1 CUP		DAILY GOAL
Calories	31	2,000 (F), 2,500 (M)
Total Fat	0 g	60 g or less (F), 70 g or less (M)
Saturated fat	0 g	20 g or less (F), 23 g or less (M)
Cholesterol	0 mg	300 mg or less
Sodium	747 mg	2,400 mg or less
Carbohydrates	5 g	250 g or more
Protein	3 g	55 g to 90 g

NOTES

CLASSIC VEGETABLE STOCK

An assortment of coarsely chopped aromatic vegetables gives this lovely broth a full-bodied flavor which makes it a great substitute for chicken broth.

▽ *Low-calorie*
   Prep time: 15 minutes
   Cooking time: 2 hours
○ *Degree of difficulty: easy*

  2 **tablespoons vegetable oil**
  2 **large onions, chopped**
  2 **ribs celery, chopped**
  4 **large carrots, peeled and chopped**
  2 **leeks (green part included), cleaned and chopped**
  8 **ounces fresh mushrooms, chopped**
  4 **garlic cloves, crushed**
 12 **cups water**
  1 **large tomato, chopped**
  4 **sprigs fresh parsley**
  1 **sprig fresh thyme *or* ½ teaspoon dried**
  1 **bay leaf**
  8 **whole peppercorns**
  2 **teaspoons salt**

1 Heat oil in a large Dutch or stockpot oven over medium-high heat. Add onions, celery, carrots, and leeks. Cook, stirring occasionally, until vegetables are just tender, 10 minutes. Add mushrooms and garlic; cook 5 minutes more.

2 Add water, tomato, parsley, thyme, bay leaf, peppercorns, and salt; bring to a boil. Reduce heat; cover and simmer 1 hour, occasionally skimming any foam from the surface. Remove from heat. Strain through a fine sieve into a large bowl; discard solids.

3 Return broth to Dutch oven; bring to a boil. Reduce heat and simmer uncovered until reduced by half, 30 minutes. (Can be made ahead. Cool. Transfer to a freezer container, cover and freeze up to 1 month.) Makes 6 cups.

PER 1 CUP		DAILY GOAL
Calories	61	2,000 (F), 2,500 (M)
Total Fat	4 g	60 g or less (F), 70 g or less (M)
Saturated fat	0 g	20 g or less (F), 23 g or less (M)
Cholesterol	0 mg	300 mg or less
Sodium	744 mg	2,400 mg or less
Carbohydrates	7 g	250 g or more
Protein	1 g	55 g to 90 g

HEARTY

MAIN COURSE

SOUPS

Sit back, relax, and stock up on hearty, chunky, satisfying meals all in one bowl. We have classic New England-style Friday Night Fish Chowder and Savory Mussel Soup with Pernod. Legumes reign supreme in Split Pea Soup with Garlic Croutons and Tuscan Bean Soup with Swiss Chard. And this collection wouldn't be complete without vegetable classics like Ukranian Cabbage Borscht and French Onion Soup topped with a crown of golden melted cheese.

CHICKEN-LIME SOUP

This light but satisfying citrus-flavored soup is based on the Latin American favorite, Sopa de Lima.

Prep time: 30 minutes
Cooking time: 1 hour 25 minutes
Degree of difficulty: easy

- 1 **whole chicken (3½ pounds), cut up**
- 1 **onion, quartered**
- 1 **carrot, peeled and coarsely chopped**
- 3 **garlic cloves, mashed**
- 7 **cups water**
  Vegetable oil
- ½ **cup finely chopped onion**
- 2 **tablespoons minced, fresh jalapeño pepper**
- 1 **can (14½ or 16 ounces) tomatoes, drained and chopped**
- 1½ **teaspoons salt**
- ½ **teaspoon freshly ground pepper**
- 3 **limes**
- 4 **corn tortillas, cut into strips**
  Fresh cilantro leaves, for garnish

1 Combine chicken, quartered onion, carrot, garlic, and water in a large Dutch oven; bring to a boil. Reduce heat and simmer 1 hour, skimming surface occasionally. Remove chicken with a slotted spoon. When meat is cool enough to handle, discard skin and bones; chop meat and set aside. Strain broth through a fine sieve into a large bowl. Discard vegetables. Skim off fat; set broth aside.

2 Heat 1 tablespoon oil in a clean Dutch oven. Add chopped onion and jalapeño; cook, stirring, over medium heat until onion is softened, 5 minutes. Add tomatoes and cook 5 minutes more. Stir in reserved chicken, chicken broth, salt, and pepper; bring to a boil. Reduce heat and simmer 10 minutes.

3 Five minutes before serving, squeeze enough juice from 2 of the limes to equal 2 tablespoons. Stir in lime juice and the shell of half a squeezed lime. Simmer 5 minutes, then discard lime shell. Thinly slice 1 remaining lime.

4 Meanwhile, heat ¼ inch oil in a small skillet over medium-high heat. Fry tortilla strips in batches until crisp, about 1 minute per batch. Drain on paper towels.

5 Spoon soup into bowls and top each with lime slices and tortilla strips. Garnish with cilantro. Makes 4 servings.

PER SERVING		DAILY GOAL	
Calories	399	2,000 (F), 2,500 (M)	
Total Fat	15 g	60 g or less (F), 70 g or less (M)	
Saturated fat	3 g	20 g or less (F), 23 g or less (M)	
Cholesterol	133 mg	300 mg or less	
Sodium	1,191 mg	2,400 mg or less	
Carbohydrates	22 g	250 g or more	
Protein	44 g	55 g to 90 g	

NOTES

_____

_____

_____

_____

_____

_____

_____

_____

_____

_____

_____

_____

GRANDMA'S CHICKEN SOUP

Nothing can replace the aroma, flavor or nostalgia of this slow-simmering homemade soup.

▽ *Low-calorie*
Prep time: 25 minutes
Cooking time: 4 hours
○ *Degree of difficulty: easy*

1 whole chicken (3½ to 4 pounds), cut up
3 quarts cold water
2 medium onions, peeled and quartered
2 carrots, peeled and cut into thirds
1 celery rib, cut into thirds
3 garlic cloves, mashed
3 fresh parsley sprigs
8 to 10 whole peppercorns
3 whole cloves
1 bay leaf
½ teaspoon thyme
1 tablespoon butter *or* margarine
2 medium carrots, peeled and diced
2 medium celery ribs, diced

1 Combine chicken and water in a large stockpot or Dutch oven; bring to a boil. Reduce heat and simmer uncovered 1 hour, occasionally skimming foam and fat off surface. Add onions, carrots, celery, garlic, parsley, peppercorns, cloves, bay leaf, and thyme. Simmer 2 hours more.

2 Remove chicken with a slotted spoon. When cool enough to handle, remove skin and bones and return to stockpot. Shred meat and set aside. Simmer broth 1 hour; strain through a fine sieve; discard solids and skim off any fat.

3 Melt butter in a small skillet over medium heat. Add carrots and celery and cook until tender, about 5 minutes. Add to broth with shredded chicken. Makes 6 servings.

PER SERVING		DAILY GOAL
Calories	211	2,000 (F), 2,500 (M)
Total Fat	6 g	60 g or less (F), 70 g or less (M)
Saturated fat	2 g	20 g or less (F), 23 g or less (M)
Cholesterol	101 mg	300 mg or less
Sodium	154 mg	2,400 mg or less
Carbohydrates	7 g	250 g or more
Protein	30 g	55 g to 90 g

CHICKEN NOODLE SOUP

Here's the soup that says "home." Use a small pasta such as orzo or ditalini.

▼ Low-fat
▽ Low-calorie
Prep time: 5 minutes
Cooking time: 20 minutes
○ Degree of difficulty: easy

2 quarts Grandma's Chicken Soup
    (recipe, page 35)
2 cups (4 ounces) fine egg noodles
¼ cup chopped fresh parsley
   Salt and freshly ground pepper

Bring Grandma's Chicken Soup to a boil in a large saucepan. Add noodles and boil until tender, 3 to 5 minutes. Stir in parsley. Season to taste with salt and pepper. Makes 6 servings.

PER SERVING		DAILY GOAL
Calories	284	2,000 (F), 2,500 (M)
Total Fat	7 g	60 g or less (F), 70 g or less (M)
Saturated fat	2 g	20 g or less (F), 23 g or less (M)
Cholesterol	118 mg	300 mg or less
Sodium	159 mg	2,400 mg or less
Carbohydrates	21 g	250 g or more
Protein	33 g	55 g to 90 g

CHICKEN-RICE SOUP

Here's a way to take advantage of leftover cooked rice!

▼ Low-fat
Prep time: 10 minutes
Cooking time: 20 minutes
○ Degree of difficulty: easy

2 quarts Grandma's Chicken Soup
    (recipe, page 35)
¼ cup white wine
3 cups cooked long-grain rice
¼ cup chopped fresh parsley
   Salt and freshly ground pepper

Bring Grandma's Chicken Soup to a boil in a large saucepan. Add white wine, rice, and parsley. Season to taste with salt and pepper. Makes 6 servings.

PER SERVING		DAILY GOAL
Calories	351	2,000 (F), 2,500 (M)
Total Fat	6 g	60 g or less (F), 70 g or less (M)
Saturated fat	2 g	20 g or less (F), 23 g or less (M)
Cholesterol	100 mg	300 mg or less
Sodium	158 mg	2,400 mg or less
Carbohydrates	36 g	250 g or more
Protein	33 g	55 g to 90 g

NOTES

CHICKEN-MATZOH BALL SOUP

This traditionally Jewish chicken soup has gained universal appeal.

▽ *Low-calorie*
   Prep time: 15 minutes
   Cooking time: 50 minutes
○ *Degree of difficulty: easy*

¼ **cup chicken fat** *or* **vegetable shortening**
4 **large eggs, lightly beaten**
1 **cup matzoh meal**
  2 teaspoons salt
¼ **cup chicken broth** *or* **water**
2 **quarts Grandma's Chicken Soup (recipe, page 35)**
½ **cup chopped fresh parsley**
  Salt and freshly ground pepper

1 Combine chicken fat and eggs in a medium bowl. Combine matzoh meal and 2 teaspoons salt in another bowl. Blend matzoh into egg mixture with chicken broth or water until smooth. Cover and refrigerate 30 minutes or up to 24 hours.

2 Bring Grandma's Chicken Soup to a boil in a large saucepan. Shape matzoh mixture into 8 balls. Drop balls, 1 at a time, into simmering broth. Reduce heat, cover, and simmer 40 minutes. Stir in parsley. Season to taste with salt and pepper. Makes 8 servings.

PER SERVING		DAILY GOAL	
Calories	320	2,000 (F), 2,500 (M)
Total Fat	14 g	60 g or less (F), 70 g or less (M)
Saturated fat	4 g	20 g or less (F), 23 g or less (M)
Cholesterol	187 mg	300 mg or less
Sodium	735 mg	2,400 mg or less
Carbohydrates	20 g	250 g or more
Protein	27 g	55 g to 90 g

NOTES

TURKEY MINESTRONE SOUP

Here's a super way to utilize economical turkey legs and thighs.

▼ *Low-fat*
▽ *Low-calorie*
  Prep time: 45 minutes plus soaking
  Cooking time: 2½ to 3 hours
○ *Degree of difficulty: easy*

1 cup Great Northern beans
  Water
2 slices bacon, diced
2 cups diced onions
1 tablespoon minced garlic
3 cups peeled, diced carrots
2 cups peeled, diced white turnips
½ teaspoon thyme
4 quarts water
2 cans (13¾ or 14½ ounces each) chicken broth or 3½ cups Rich Chicken Stock (recipe, page 29)
2 pounds raw turkey legs or thighs, skin removed
1 bay leaf
4 teaspoons salt
½ teaspoon freshly ground pepper
1 cup ditalini or small elbow macaroni, cooked according to package directions and rinsed
1 head escarole, chopped
  Grated Parmesan cheese

1 Rinse beans and pick over for small stones and shriveled beans. In a large bowl, cover beans with 2 inches water and soak overnight. (To quick-soak: Combine beans with water to cover by 2 inches in a large saucepan and bring to a boil; boil 2 minutes. Cover and let stand 1 hour.) Drain in a colander; set aside.

2 Cook bacon in a large Dutch oven over medium-high heat until crisp. Add onions and garlic; cook, stirring, until onions are softened, about 3 minutes. Add carrots, turnips, and thyme; cook 1 minute. Add water, chicken broth, turkey, bay leaf, salt, and pepper; bring to a boil. Reduce heat and simmer uncovered 1 hour, skimming occasionally foam and fat from surface.

3 Remove turkey with a slotted spoon and transfer to a plate. When cool enough to handle, remove and discard bones. Dice or shred meat and return to pot. Add beans; bring to a boil. Reduce heat and simmer uncovered until beans are tender, 1½ hours.

4 Add cooked ditalini and escarole; cook until escarole is tender, 5 minutes. Remove bay leaf. Spoon into bowls and serve with grated Parmesan. Makes 10 servings.

PER SERVING		DAILY GOAL
Calories	236	2,000 (F), 2,500 (M)
Total Fat	6 g	60 g or less (F), 70 g or less (M)
Saturated fat	2 g	20 g or less (F), 23 g or less (M)
Cholesterol	37mg	300 mg or less
Sodium	1,399 mg	2,400 mg or less
Carbohydrates	29 g	250 g or more
Protein	17 g	55 g to 90 g

NOTES

_____

_____

_____

_____

_____

_____

_____

_____

_____

MEXICAN MEATBALL SOUP

No need to brown these tender turkey meatballs spiked with jalapeño and cilantro because they cook right in the simmering soup! *Also pictured on page 32.*

▽ *Low-calorie*
Prep time: 30 minutes
Cooking time: 25 minutes
○ *Degree of difficulty: easy*

- 8 ounces ground turkey
- ¾ cup fresh bread crumbs
- 1 large egg
- 2 tablespoons chopped fresh cilantro
- 2 tablespoons seeded and minced jalapeño peppers, divided
- 2 teaspoons minced garlic, divided
- ½ teaspoon salt
- ⅛ teaspoon ground red pepper
- 1 tablespoon vegetable oil
- ½ cup finely chopped onion
- 1 can (14½ or 16 ounces) tomatoes, drained and chopped
- 2 cans (13¾ or 14½ ounces each) chicken broth or 3½ cups Rich Chicken Stock (recipe, page 29)
- 2 cups water
- 1 cup frozen whole-kernel corn
- 2 tablespoon fresh lime juice
- ½ teaspoon freshly ground pepper
- 1 avocado, peeled, seeded, and diced
  Fresh cilantro leaves, for garnish

1 For meatballs, combine turkey, bread crumbs, egg, cilantro, 1 tablespoon of the jalapeño, 1 teaspoon of the garlic, salt, and red pepper in a medium bowl and mix well. Shape into 1-inch balls.

2 For soup, heat oil in a large saucepan over medium heat. Add onion and remaining 1 tablespoon jalapeño and cook until onion is softened, 5 minutes. Stir in tomatoes, remaining 1 teaspoon garlic, chicken broth, and water. Increase heat and bring to a boil. Add meatballs and return to a boil.

3 Reduce heat, cover, and simmer soup 10 minutes. Add corn, lime juice, and pepper; simmer 5 minutes more. Spoon soup into bowls and top each with avocado and cilantro. Makes 6 servings.

PER SERVING		DAILY GOAL
Calories	225	2,000 (F), 2,500 (M)
Total Fat	13 g	60 g or less (F), 70 g or less (M)
Saturated fat	2 g	20 g or less (F), 23 g or less (M)
Cholesterol	63 mg	300 mg or less
Sodium	1,067 mg	2,400 mg or less
Carbohydrates	17 g	250 g or more
Protein	12 g	55 g to 90 g

NOTES

HAMBURGER SOUP

It's hard to believe that such a hearty, flavorful soup could be so quick and easy!

▼ *Low-fat*
▽ *Low-calorie*
  Prep time: 10 minutes
  Cooking time: 32 minutes
O *Degree of difficulty: easy*

1 **pound lean (95%) ground beef**
1 **tablespoon vegetable oil**
1 **cup diced carrots**
1 **cup diced onions**
1 **cup sliced celery**
½ **teaspoon minced garlic**
2 **cans (13¾ *or* 14½ ounces each) chicken broth *or* 3½ cups Rich Chicken Stock (recipe, page 29)**
1 **can (14½ *or* 16 ounces) tomatoes, liquid reserved**
½ **teaspoon thyme**
½ **teaspoon salt**
¼ **teaspoon freshly ground pepper**
3 **cups (4 ounces) wide egg noodles, cooked according to package directions**

¼ **cup chopped fresh parsley**
  Sour cream, for garnish

1 Cook ground beef in a large Dutch oven over medium-high heat until browned, 5 to 7 minutes. Remove meat from pan with a slotted spoon and set aside.

2 Add oil, carrots, onions, celery, and garlic to pan; cook until tender-crisp, 5 minutes. Carefully add chicken broth, tomatoes, thyme, salt, pepper, and beef, breaking up tomatoes with the back of a spoon; bring to a boil. Reduce heat, cover and simmer 20 minutes.

3 Just before serving, stir noodles and parsley into soup and heat through. Spoon into bowls and garnish each with a dollop of sour cream. Makes 4 servings.

PER SERVING WITHOUT SOUR CREAM		DAILY GOAL
Calories	233	2,000 (F), 2,500 (M)
Total Fat	7 g	60 g or less (F), 70 g or less (M)
Saturated fat	1 g	20 g or less (F), 23 g or less (M)
Cholesterol	55 mg	300 mg or less
Sodium	1,169 mg	2,400 mg or less
Carbohydrates	24 g	250 g or more
Protein	19 g	55 g to 90 g

CHICK-PEA AND CHORIZO SOUP

Garlicky chorizo sausage is a favorite in Mexican cooking, and it gives this pea soup a rich south-of-the-border flavor. Be sure to remove the sausage casing before chopping the chorizo.

▽ *Low-calorie*
Prep time: 10 minutes
Cooking time: 20 minutes
O *Degree of difficulty: easy*

4 **ounces chorizo sausage, finely chopped**
½ **cup chopped onion**
⅓ **cup chopped green pepper**
1 **garlic clove, minced**
1 **can (19 ounces) chick-peas (garbanzo beans), drained and rinsed**
1 **can (13¾ *or* 14½ ounces) chicken broth *or* 1¾ cups Rich Chicken Stock (recipe, page 29)**
1 **cup water**
¼ **cup chopped tomato**
1 **tablespoon chopped fresh cilantro Diced avocado, for garnish**

1 Combine chorizo, onion, green pepper, and garlic in a medium saucepan. Cook over medium-high heat until sausage is browned and vegetables are tender, 5 minutes. Drain fat from pan.

2 Stir in chick-peas, chicken broth, water, and tomato; bring to a boil. Reduce heat and simmer 15 minutes. Stir in cilantro. Spoon into bowls and top with avocado. Makes 2 or 3 servings.

PER SERVING		DAILY GOAL
Calories	338	2,000 (F), 2,500 (M)
Total Fat	14 g	60 g or less (F), 70 g or less (M)
Saturated fat	4 g	20 g or less (F), 23 g or less (M)
Cholesterol	22 mg	300 mg or less
Sodium	1,670 mg	2,400 mg or less
Carbohydrates	34 g	250 g or more
Protein	18 g	55 g to 90 g

CALDO VERDE

This classic "green soup" from Portugal features fresh kale, potatoes, and a spicy linguiça sausage. Chorizo or kielbasa sausage make fine substitutes.

▽ *Low-calorie*
  Prep time: 20 minutes
  Cooking time: 45 minutes
○ *Degree of difficulty: easy*

2 **tablespoons olive oil**
2 **cups chopped onions**
2 **teaspoons minced garlic**
2 **cans (13¾ *or* 14½ ounces each) chicken broth *or* 3½ cups Rich Chicken Stock (recipe, page 29) Water**
3 **pounds potatoes, peeled and thinly sliced**
1 **pound kale, large stems removed, shredded**
4 **ounces linguiça, chorizo, *or* kielbasa sausage, pierced with a fork**
1 **teaspoon salt**
¼ **teaspoon freshly ground pepper**

1 Heat oil over medium heat in a large Dutch oven. Add onions and garlic; cover and cook, stirring occasionally, until softened, about 5 minutes. Add chicken broth, 4 cups water, and potatoes; cover and bring to a boil. Reduce heat and simmer until potatoes are tender, 20 minutes. Add kale and simmer uncovered 10 minutes.

2 Meanwhile, cook sausage with 2 cups boiling water in a small saucepan 5 minutes. Drain and cool slightly. Remove sausage from casings and chop.

3 Transfer 2 cups potato mixture to a food processor and puree until smooth. Return puree to remaining soup; add sausage, salt, and pepper. Simmer 5 minutes. Makes 7 servings.

PER SERVING		DAILY GOAL
Calories	256	2,000 (F), 2,500 (M)
Total Fat	10 g	60 g or less (F), 70 g or less (M)
Saturated fat	2 g	20 g or less (F), 23 g or less (M)
Cholesterol	10 mg	300 mg or less
Sodium	1,100 mg	2,400 mg or less
Carbohydrates	36 g	250 g or more
Protein	8 g	55 g to 90 g

NOTES

SCOTCH BROTH

This classic soup of lamb and barley from the British Isles is cooked in one pot without browning.

▼   *Low-fat*
▽   *Low-calorie*
    Prep time: 20 minutes plus chilling
    Cooking time: about 2 hours
○   *Degree of difficulty: easy*

3   pounds meaty lamb neck bones
9   cups water
1   onion, chopped
1½   teaspoons salt
½   teaspoon freshly ground pepper
¼   teaspoon thyme
½   cup pearl barley
1   cup frozen peas
3   carrots, peeled and julienned
1   turnip, peeled and julienned
1   leek, julienned
2   tablespoons chopped fresh parsley

1 Combine lamb, water, onion, salt, pepper, and thyme in a large Dutch oven; bring to a boil. Reduce heat and simmer uncovered 1 hour. Add barley and simmer 1 hour more. Remove from heat and cool to room temperature. Cover and refrigerate overnight.

2 Skim fat from surface of soup. Remove meat from bones; discard bones. Chop meat and return to soup. Heat to boiling. Add peas, carrots, turnip, and leek. Cover and simmer until vegetables are tender, 10 minutes. Stir in parsley and spoon into soup bowls. Makes 6 servings.

PER SERVING		DAILY GOAL
Calories	178	2,000 (F), 2,500 (M)
Total Fat	3 g	60 g or less (F), 70 g or less (M)
Saturated fat	1 g	20 g or less (F), 23 g or less (M)
Cholesterol	25 mg	300 mg or less
Sodium	634 mg	2,400 mg or less
Carbohydrates	26 g	250 g or more
Protein	11 g	55 g to 90 g

NOTES

SEAFOOD AND FENNEL CHOWDER

Fresh fennel does wonders for this soup. Its subtle flavor brings out the sweetness of seafood. You can substitute celery, but fennel is now available year around, although its peak season is from December to April.

▽ *Low-calorie*
Prep time: 20 minutes
Cooking time: 25 minutes
O *Degree of difficulty: easy*

1 tablespoon butter *or* margarine
½ cup finely chopped onion
1 large fennel bulb, cored and sliced (2¼ cups)
1 pound new potatoes, diced
2 cups peeled, diagonally sliced carrots
2 bottles (8 ounces each) clam juice
1 cup water
1 teaspoon salt
¼ teaspoon freshly ground pepper
Pinch thyme
1 pound cod fillet, cut into chunks

4 ounces shrimp, peeled and deveined
½ cup heavy *or* whipping cream
¼ cup chopped fresh parsley

1 Melt butter in a large saucepan over medium-low heat. Add onion and fennel and cook, stirring occasionally, until tender, 10 minutes. Add potatoes, carrots, clam juice, water, salt, pepper, and thyme; bring to a boil. Reduce heat, cover, and simmer until vegetables are just tender, 10 minutes.

2 Add cod and shrimp to pot. Cover and simmer until seafood turns opaque, 5 minutes. Gently stir in cream and cook just until heated through (*do not boil*). Sprinkle with parsley. Makes 6 servings.

PER SERVING		DAILY GOAL
Calories	250	2,000 (F), 2,500 (M)
Total Fat	10 g	60 g or less (F), 70 g or less (M)
Saturated fat	5 g	20 g or less (F), 23 g or less (M)
Cholesterol	88 mg	300 mg or less
Sodium	687 mg	2,400 mg or less
Carbohydrates	20 g	250 g or more
Protein	20 g	55 g to 90 g

47

OYSTER CHOWDER WITH SPINACH

We've lightened up this classic seafood soup and added shredded fresh spinach and other healthful veggies. Serve with toasted pita bread pieces for a change of pace from oyster crackers.

▽ *Low-calorie*
Prep time: 15 minutes
Cooking time: 20 minutes
○ *Degree of difficulty: easy*

1 **tablespoon olive oil**
½ **cup finely chopped celery**
½ **cup minced shallots**
1 **tablespoon all-purpose flour**
3 **bottles (8 ounces each) clam juice**
1 **pint fresh shucked oysters (about 2 dozen), strained, liquor reserved**
2 **large potatoes, peeled and diced**
1 **cup low-fat (1%) milk**
¼ **teaspoon salt**
¼ **teaspoon freshly ground pepper**
4 **cups packed fresh spinach leaves (5 ounces), cut into ½-inch-thick strips**

1 Heat oil in a large saucepan over medium heat. Add celery and shallots; cook until softened, 4 minutes. Stir in flour until blended, then stir in clam juice and reserved oyster liquor. Bring to a boil.

2 Add potatoes; reduce heat and simmer until potatoes are very tender, 15 minutes. Stir in milk, salt, and pepper. Add oysters and simmer until cooked through, about 2 minutes more. Stir in the spinach and continue cooking until wilted, 1 minute. Immediately spoon soup into bowls. Makes 8 servings.

PER SERVING		DAILY GOAL
Calories	123	2,000 (F), 2,500 (M)
Total Fat	4 g	60 g or less (F), 70 g or less (M)
Saturated fat	1 g	20 g or less (F), 23 g or less (M)
Cholesterol	36 mg	300 mg or less
Sodium	371 mg	2,400 mg or less
Carbohydrates	15 g	250 g or more
Protein	8 g	55 g to 90 g

FISH SUBSTITUTES

Can't find a fish fillet called for in a recipe? When it comes to these soups and stews, it's often possible to make a switch.

• **Cod (Scrod):** Delicate, white, and firm-textured. Alternatives: haddock, flounder, pollock, pike, hake, halibut.

• **Monkfish:** Light-colored, firm texture; sweet flavor similar to lobster. Alternatives: grouper, tilefish, halibut.

• **Red Snapper:** Medium flavor, light-colored with a soft texture. Alternatives: sea bass, sea trout, sole, catfish.

• **Sea Bass:** Flavorful, white, and firm texture. Alternatives: orange roughy, sea trout, red snapper, halibut.

• **Catfish:** White, firm texture, and bony. Alternatives: red snapper, whitefish, sole, perch.

• **Halibut:** Meaty white fish with a sweet flavor. Alternatives: cod, tilefish, sea bass.

NEW ENGLAND CLAM AND COD CHOWDER

We've lightly mashed the potatoes to give this hearty clam chowder extra body and creaminess.

▽ *Low-calorie*
   Prep time: 20 minutes
   Cooking time: 35 minutes
○ *Degree of difficulty: easy*

2 **dozen cherrystone clams, scrubbed and rinsed**
   Water
4 **ounces bacon, diced**
1 **cup chopped onions**
3 **cups peeled, diced potatoes**
1 **bottle (8 ounces) clam juice**
½ **teaspoon freshly ground pepper**
   Pinch thyme
1 **pound cod fillet, cut into 1-inch pieces**
⅓ **cup heavy *or* whipping cream**
1 **tablespoon chopped fresh parsley**

1 Combine clams and ½ cup cold water in a large Dutch oven; cover and bring to a boil. Steam over high heat 6 minutes. With a slotted spoon, transfer any open clams to a medium bowl. Continue steaming remaining clams until they open (discard any that remain closed after 5 to 7 minutes). Reserve liquid. Remove clams from shells; chop coarsely and set aside. Strain liquid through a sieve lined with cheesecloth into a 2-cup measure and add enough water to equal 2 cups. Set aside.

2 Cook bacon in a clean Dutch oven until crisp. Remove with a slotted spoon; drain on paper towels. Pour off all but 1 tablespoon drippings. Add onions and cook over medium heat until softened, 10 minutes. Add reserved clam liquid, potatoes, clam juice, pepper, and thyme; bring to a boil. Reduce heat and simmer until potatoes are very tender, 20 minutes.

3 Lightly mash potatoes with a hand masher. Add reserved chopped clams and cod and cook partially covered 5 minutes more. Stir in cream *(do not boil)*. Adjust seasonings; sprinkle with reserved bacon and parsley. Immediately spoon soup into bowls. Makes 6 servings.

PER SERVING		DAILY GOAL
Calories	268	2,000 (F), 2,500 (M)
Total Fat	10 g	60 g or less (F), 70 g or less (M)
Saturated fat	5 g	20 g or less (F), 23 g or less (M)
Cholesterol	77 mg	300 mg or less
Sodium	266 mg	2,400 mg or less
Carbohydrates	18 g	250 g or more
Protein	25 g	55 g to 90 g

NOTES

_____

_____

_____

_____

_____

_____

_____

_____

_____

_____

_____

_____

_____

FRIDAY NIGHT FISH CHOWDER

This is home cooking! Plus, you can cook most of this New England-style soup ahead of time.

▽ *Low-calorie*
Prep time: 20 minutes
Cooking time: 45 minutes
○ *Degree of difficulty: easy*

3 **slices bacon, chopped**
1 **cup finely chopped onions**
¼ **cup all-purpose flour**
1 **bottle (8 ounces) clam juice**
1 **cup water**
1 **teaspoon salt**
½ **teaspoon freshly ground pepper**
½ **teaspoon thyme**
¼ **teaspoon red pepper sauce**
8 **ounces red potatoes, diced in**
    ¾-inch pieces (3 cups)
1 **pound cod *or* scrod fillet, cut into**
    ¾-inch cubes
2 **cups milk**
2 **tablespoons chopped fresh parsley**

1 Cook bacon in a large saucepan over medium heat until crisp; drain on paper towels. Pour off all but 1 tablespoon of drippings from the pan. Add onions and cook until softened, about 5 minutes. Stir in flour until blended and cook, stirring, 1 minute.

2 Gradually whisk in clam juice, water, salt, pepper, thyme, and pepper sauce. Bring to a boil, whisking constantly. Add potatoes, then reduce heat and simmer until potatoes are very tender, 25 minutes. (Can be made ahead. Return soup to a simmer before adding fish.)

3 Add fish and cook until just opaque, 2 to 3 minutes. Stir in milk and continue to cook until just heated through. Immediately spoon soup into bowls and sprinkle with reserved bacon and parsley. Makes 4 servings.

PER SERVING		DAILY GOAL
Calories	310	2,000 (F), 2,500 (M)
Total Fat	10 g	60 g or less (F), 70 g or less (M)
Saturated fat	4 g	20 g or less (F), 23 g or less (M)
Cholesterol	72 mg	300 mg or less
Sodium	907 mg	2,400 mg or less
Carbohydrates	26 g	250 g or more
Protein	28 g	55 g to 90 g

SAVORY MUSSEL SOUP WITH PERNOD

Always be sure to purchase mussels with tightly closed shells or those that snap shut when tapped, so you know they are alive and fresh. Mussels must be thoroughly cleaned before cooking. Scrub the shells with a stiff brush under cold running water, then with a small sharp knife, remove and discard the "beards" (the small black tufts attached to the shells).

Prep time: 30 minutes
Cooking time: 30 to 35 minutes
Degree of difficulty: moderate

4   **bottles (8 ounces each) clam juice, divided**
1   **cup white wine**
1   **large bunch fresh parsley, coarsely chopped**
8   **garlic cloves, pressed**
4   **pounds fresh mussels, scrubbed, rinsed, and cleaned**
½   **cup butter *or* margarine**
2   **cups chopped onions**
1½ **cups peeled, chopped carrots**
1   **cup chopped celery**
1½ **teaspoons fennel seed**
½   **teaspoon thyme**
1½ **cups heavy *or* whipping cream**
1   **tablespoon pernod *or* ouzo**

1 Mix 1 bottle of the clam juice, wine, parsley, and garlic and bring to a boil in a large saucepan. Add mussels, cover, and steam over high heat 5 minutes. With a slotted spoon, transfer any open mussels to a medium bowl. Continue steaming remaining mussels until they open (discard any that remain closed after 5 to 7 minutes). Remove mussels from shells and set aside. Reserve mussel broth.

2 Melt butter in the same saucepan over medium heat. Add onions, carrots, and celery; cook until vegetables are tender, about 10 minutes. Stir in remaining 3 bottles clam juice, fennel seed, and thyme and simmer 15 minutes. Add reserved mussel broth. Puree soup in a blender in small batches, then strain through a fine sieve into a bowl. Return to saucepan and stir in cream, pernod, and reserved mussels. Cook until just heated through. Immediately spoon soup into bowls. Makes 6 servings.

PER SERVING		DAILY GOAL
Calories	503	2,000 (F), 2,500 (M)
Total Fat	40 g	60 g or less (F), 70 g or less (M)
Saturated fat	24 g	20 g or less (F), 23 g or less (M)
Cholesterol	147 mg	300 mg or less
Sodium	813 mg	2,400 mg or less
Carbohydrates	17 g	250 g or more
Protein	14 g	55 g to 90 g

NOTES

51

UKRAINIAN CABBAGE BORSCHT

Although you can find many hot and cold versions of this hearty soup, it's always prepared with fresh beets and garnished with a dollop of sour cream.

▽   *Low-calorie*
    Prep time: 30 minutes plus chilling
    Cooking time: 2 hours 35 minutes
○   *Degree of difficulty: easy*

3½ **pounds beef short ribs**
1   **large beef bone**
4½ **cups water**
2   **cans (13¾ *or* 14½ ounces each) beef broth *or* 3½ cups Hearty Beef Stock (recipe, page 30)**
2   **onions, diced**
1   **can (14½ *or* 16 ounces) tomatoes, chopped and liquid reserved**
3   **carrots, peeled and sliced**
1   **celery rib, sliced**
1   **tablespoon salt**
¾   **teaspoon freshly ground pepper**
4   **cups coarsely shredded beets**

2   **pounds finely shredded cabbage (about 8 cups)**
1   **tablespoon sugar**
2   **tablespoons fresh lemon juice**
1   **cup sour cream**
¼   **cup chopped fresh dill *or* 1 tablespoon dillweed**

1   Combine short ribs, soup bone, water, and beef broth in a large saucepan; bring to a boil. Add onions, tomatoes, carrots, celery, salt, and pepper; simmer uncovered 1 hour.

2   Remove ribs with a slotted spoon, leaving soup bone. When ribs are cool enough to handle, cut meat into bite-size pieces and return meat to saucepan. Discard bones and fat. Add beets; partially cover and simmer 1 hour. Discard soup bone. Cool, then refrigerate several hours or overnight. Skim fat from surface of soup and discard.

3   Return soup to a boil, stirring occasionally. Add cabbage and until cabbage is tender about 35 minutes. Add sugar and lemon juice. Spoon soup into bowls and top each with a dollop of sour cream and sprinkle with dill. Makes 10 servings.

PER SERVING		DAILY GOAL
Calories	253	2,000 (F), 2,500 (M)
Total Fat	12 g	60 g or less (F), 70 g or less (M)
Saturated fat	6 g	20 g or less (F), 23 g or less (M)
Cholesterol	49 mg	300 mg or less
Sodium	1,223 mg	2,400 mg or less
Carbohydrates	20 g	250 g or more
Protein	17 g	55 g to 90 g

NOTES

ECUADOREAN POTATO SOUP

Paprika is the key spice in this Latin American soup, which is made rich and creamy by the addition of shredded muenster cheese.

▽ *Low-calorie*
Prep time: 30 minutes
Cooking time: 45 minutes
○ *Degree of difficulty: easy*

3 tablespoons butter *or* margarine, divided
1½ cups diced onions, divided
1 tablespoon paprika
2 cans (13¾ *or* 14½ ounces each) chicken broth *or* 3½ cups Rich Chicken Stock (recipe, page 29)
4 cups water
4 pounds baking potatoes, peeled and sliced
1 cup milk
2 cups (about 8 ounces) shredded muenster cheese
1 teaspoon salt, divided
½ teaspoon freshly ground pepper, divided
1 package (10 ounces) frozen whole-kernel corn, thawed
1 can (16 ounces) tomatoes, drained and chopped

1 Melt 2 tablespoons of the butter in a large Dutch oven over medium-high heat. Add 1 cup of the onions and paprika and cook until onions are softened, 5 minutes. Add chicken broth, water, and potatoes; bring to a boil. Reduce heat and simmer uncovered until potatoes are tender, 30 minutes.

2 Lightly mash potatoes with a hand masher. Stir in milk, cheese, ½ teaspoon of the salt, and ¼ teaspoon of the pepper. Cook over medium heat, stirring occasionally, until cheese is melted.

3 Meanwhile, melt the remaining 1 tablespoon butter in a small skillet over medium-high heat. Add remaining ½ cup onions and cook 1 minute. Add corn and tomatoes and cook until heated through. Stir in remaining ½ teaspoon salt and remaining ¼ teaspoon pepper. Spoon soup into bowls and top each with 2 tablespoons corn and tomato mixture. Makes 12 servings.

PER SERVING		DAILY GOAL	
Calories	245	2,000 (F), 2,500 (M)	
Total Fat	10 g	60 g or less (F), 70 g or less (M)	
Saturated fat	6 g	20 g or less (F), 23 g or less (M)	
Cholesterol	29 mg	300 mg or less	
Sodium	752 mg	2,400 mg or less	
Carbohydrates	31 g	250 g or more	
Protein	9 g	55 g to 90 g	

NOTES

_____

_____

_____

_____

_____

_____

_____

_____

_____

_____

_____

_____

_____

_____

_____

_____

CLASSIC FRENCH ONION SOUP

You'll need a heavy skillet, because the secret of this soup's rich flavor is slowly cooking the onions with just a touch of sugar until they turn a dark caramel brown. The golden cheese topping features Gruyère, an imported Swiss, and freshly grated Parmesan cheese.

Prep time: 25 minutes
Cooking time: 65 to 70 minutes
○ *Degree of difficulty: easy*

¼ **cup unsalted butter**
    (no substitutions)
2 **tablespoons vegetable oil**
2½ **pounds onions, thinly sliced**
1½ **teaspoons sugar**
4 **cans (13¾ *or* 14½ ounces each)**
    beef broth *or* 7 cups Hearty Beef
    Stock (recipe, page 30), divided
1¼ **cups water**
2 **bay leaves**
15 **to 20 whole peppercorns**
¾ **cup cognac *or* brandy**
8 **ounces Gruyère cheese, grated**
8 **ounces Parmesan cheese, grated**
6 **slices French bread, cut ¼ inch**
    thick

1 Heat butter and oil over medium-high heat in a large heavy skillet until bubbly, but not browned. Add onions and sprinkle with sugar, stirring to prevent scorching. Reduce heat and cook onions, stirring occasionally, until very tender and a deep golden brown, about 20 to 30 minutes.

2 Carefully stir in 1 can of the beef broth (or 1¾ cups Hearty Beef Stock), scraping up the browned bits from bottom of pan. Transfer to a 3-quart saucepan. Add remaining 3 cans beef broth (or 5¼ cups Hearty Beef Stock), water, bay leaves, and peppercorns; bring to a boil. Reduce heat and simmer 30 minutes. Add cognac and simmer 5 minutes more. Remove bay leaves from the soup.

3 Preheat broiler. Toast bread lightly on both sides. Combine cheeses in a medium bowl. Divide soup and onions evenly among six, 1½-cup oven-proof bowls. Float one slice of toast on top of each bowl. Sprinkle tops with cheese, completely covering toast, and immediately place under the broiler. (If allowed to sit, the cheese and bread will sink to the bottom.) Broil until cheese is melted and a deep golden brown, 1 to 2 minutes. Makes 6 servings.

PER SERVING		DAILY GOAL
Calories	645	2,000 (F), 2,500 (M)
Total Fat	37 g	60 g or less (F), 70 g or less (M)
Saturated fat	20 g	20 g or less (F), 23 g or less (M)
Cholesterol	92 mg	300 mg or less
Sodium	2,150 mg	2,400 mg or less
Carbohydrates	27 g	250 g or more
Protein	33 g	55 g to 90 g

NOTES

55

TUSCAN BEAN SOUP WITH SWISS CHARD

Chard is available with either red or green leaves and can be prepared like spinach, but be sure to remove the tough stalks.

▼ *Low-fat*
▽ *Low-calorie*
  Prep time: 40 minutes plus standing
  Cooking time: 2½ to 3 hours
○ *Degree of difficulty: moderate*

- 1 **pound dried white beans (cannellini or Great Northern)**
- 2 **pounds crosscut beef shank or chuck arm roast**
- 2¼ **teaspoons salt, divided**
- ½ **teaspoon freshly ground pepper, divided**
- 2 **tablespoons olive oil, divided**
- 3 **cups chopped onions**
- 3 **cups peeled, chopped carrots**
- 2 **cups chopped fennel or celery**
- 1 **tablespoon minced garlic**
- ½ **bay leaf**
- 1 **tablespoon chopped fresh thyme or ½ teaspoon dried**
- 2 **teaspoons chopped fresh rosemary or ¼ teaspoon dried**

- 2 **smoked ham hocks (about 1½ pounds)**
- 8 **cups water**
- 2 **cans (13¾ or 14½ ounces each) chicken broth or 3½ cups Rich Chicken Stock (recipe, page 29) or Hearty Beef Stock (recipe, page 30)**
- 1 **can (14½ or 16 ounces) tomatoes, drained and coarsely chopped**
- 8 **cups sliced Swiss chard or torn spinach**

1 Rinse beans and pick over for small stones and shriveled beans. In a large bowl, cover beans with 2 inches water and soak overnight. (To quick-soak: Combine beans with water to cover by 2 inches in a large saucepan and bring to a boil; boil 2 minutes. Cover and let stand 1 hour.) Drain in a colander; set aside.

2 Remove beef from bone and cut into ½-inch cubes. Sprinkle beef and beef bone with ¼ teaspoon of the salt and ¼ teaspoon of the pepper. Heat 1 tablespoon of the oil in large Dutch oven over high heat. Add beef and bone in 2 batches and cook until browned on all sides, 5 minutes per batch. Transfer to a plate with a slotted spoon.

3 Heat remaining 1 tablespoon oil in Dutch oven over medium-high heat. Add onions, carrots, and fennel. Cover and cook, stirring occasionally, until vegetables are tender, 10 minutes. Stir in garlic, bay leaf, thyme, and rosemary; cook 30 seconds. Return beef and bone to Dutch oven; add drained beans, ham hocks, water, chicken broth, remaining 2 teaspoons salt and remaining ¼ teaspoon pepper; bring to boil. Reduce heat and simmer, partially covered, 1 hour. Stir in tomatoes. Simmer until beans and meats are tender, 30 minutes more.

4 Remove ham hocks and cool. Cut meat into ½-inch pieces and return to soup. Discard all bones and bay leaf. (Can be made ahead. Cool. Cover and refrigerate soup up to 2 days.) Skim fat. Return soup to a simmer, then stir in chard and cook until chard is tender, 10 minutes. (If soup is too thick, add 1 more can chicken broth or 1¾ cups homemade stock.) Makes 12 servings.

PER SERVING		DAILY GOAL
Calories	300	2,000 (F), 2,500 (M)
Total Fat	8 g	60 g or less (F), 70 g or less (M)
Saturated fat	2 g	20 g or less (F), 23 g or less (M)
Cholesterol	28 mg	300 mg or less
Sodium	1,056 mg	2,400 mg or less
Carbohydrates	33 g	250 g or more
Protein	24 g	55 g to 90 g

57

LEAN BEAN AND CORN CHOWDER

Smoky baked ham and just a touch of oil packs a flavor punch without adding a lot of fat and calories.

▼ *Low-fat*
▽ *Low-calorie*
   Prep time: 5 minutes
   Cooking time: 6 minutes
○ *Degree of difficulty: easy*

1 teaspoon vegetable oil
4 ounces diced baked ham *or* sliced
   chorizo sausage
1 medium onion, chopped
1 clove garlic, chopped
1 teaspoon cumin
¼ teaspoon oregano
1 can (13¾ *or* 14½ ounces) chicken
   broth *or* 1¾ cups Rich Chicken
   Stock (recipe, page 29)
1 can (17 ounces) corn, drained and
   rinsed
2 cans (15 *or* 15½ ounces each) black
   beans, drained and rinsed,
   divided

½ cup water
¼ cup chopped fresh cilantro
¼ teaspoon freshly ground pepper

1 Heat oil in a large saucepan over high heat. Add ham and brown, stirring, 2 minutes. Stir in onion and garlic and cook 1 minute. Stir in cumin and oregano, cook 30 seconds until fragrant. Add chicken broth, corn, and ½ cup of the beans to saucepan.

2 Puree remaining beans with water in a blender until smooth; stir into soup. Cover and bring to a boil. Reduce heat and simmer, covered, 2 minutes. Stir in cilantro and pepper. Makes 4 servings.

PER SERVING		DAILY GOAL
Calories	300	2,000 (F), 2,500 (M)
Total Fat	7 g	60 g or less (F), 70 g or less (M)
Saturated fat	1 g	20 g or less (F), 23 g or less (M)
Cholesterol	16 mg	300 mg or less
Sodium	1,615 mg	2,400 mg or less
Carbohydrates	46 g	250 g or more
Protein	18 g	55 g to 90 g

COOKING PERFECT BEANS

• Pick over dried beans carefully and remove any small stones or shriveled beans.

• Soak dried beans. It cuts the cooking time in half and improves the texture of the cooked beans.

• To retain the whole shape of the beans and keep them tender, gently simmer the beans over medium-low heat.

• Salt or anything acidic—such as tomatoes, wine, vinegar, or chilies—will toughen the beans during cooking. Always add these ingredients after the beans are cooked and tender.

• If you wish to substitute canned beans for fresh, one 14- or 16-ounce can will equal approximately 2 cups of cooked beans or ⅔ cup dried. Drain and rinse the canned beans before using, and add them during the last 15 minutes of cooking, or just long enough to heat them through.

FRENCH CABBAGE AND BEAN SOUP

This peasant soup, called Garbure, is from the Basque region of France.

▼ *Low-fat*
▽ *Low-calorie*
   Prep time: 30 minutes plus soaking
   Cooking time: 2 hours
○ *Degree of difficulty: easy*

2   **cups Great Northern beans**
     Water
2   **smoked ham hocks**
        (about 1½ pounds)
1   **teaspoon crushed red pepper**
½   **teaspoon marjoram**
½   **teaspoon thyme**
1   **bay leaf**
3   **sprigs fresh parsley**
2   **pounds green cabbage, sliced into**
        1-inch strips
1½   **pounds potatoes, peeled and cubed**
1½   **pounds peeled carrots, sliced**
1   **pound peeled white turnips, cubed**
1   **cup chopped onions**
8   **ounces smoked ham, cubed**
1   **tablespoon minced garlic**

2   **teaspoons salt**
½   **teaspoon freshly ground pepper**

1 Rinse beans and pick over for small stones and shriveled beans. In a large bowl, cover beans with 2 inches water and soak overnight. (To quick-soak: Combine beans with water to cover by 2 inches in a large saucepan and bring to a boil; boil 2 minutes. Cover and let stand 1 hour.) Drain in a colander; set aside.

2 Combine beans with 4 quarts water, ham hocks, red pepper, marjoram, thyme, bay leaf, and parsley; bring to a boil. Reduce heat and simmer uncovered 1 hour.

3 Stir in cabbage, potatoes, carrots, turnips, onions, ham, garlic, salt, and pepper. Return to a simmer and cook 1 hour more, occasionally skimming foam and fat from surface. Remove ham hocks. Remove meat from bones; discard skin and bones. Shred meat and return to soup. Makes 12 servings.

PER SERVING		DAILY GOAL
Calories	247	2,000 (F), 2,500 (M)
Total Fat	3 g	60 g or less (F), 70 g or less (M)
Saturated fat	1 g	20 g or less (F), 23 g or less (M)
Cholesterol	18 mg	300 mg or less
Sodium	974 mg	2,400 mg or less
Carbohydrates	41 g	250 g or more
Protein	17 g	55 g to 90 g

59

GOOD OLD HAM AND BEAN SOUP

We call for Great Northern beans in this trusty stand-by, but cannellini or navy beans would do the job well, too.

▼ *Low-fat*
   Prep time: 30 minutes plus soaking
   Cooking time: 2½ hours
O *Degree of difficulty: easy*

1 **pound Great Northern beans**
   Water
2 **smoked ham hocks**
       (about 1½ pounds)
1 **slice bacon, diced**
3 **medium onions, finely chopped**
2 **celery ribs, finely chopped**
3 **garlic cloves, finely minced**
½ **cup chopped fresh parsley**
1 **teaspoon salt**
¼ **teaspoon freshly ground pepper**
1 **tablespoon white vinegar**

1 Rinse beans and pick over for small stones and shriveled beans. In a large bowl, cover beans with 2 inches water and soak overnight. (To quick-soak: Combine beans with water to cover by 2 inches in a large saucepan and bring to a boil; boil 2 minutes. Cover and let stand 1 hour.) Drain in a colander.

2 Combine beans, 2 quarts water, and ham hocks in a large Dutch oven. Cover and bring to a boil. Reduce heat to a simmer.

3 Meanwhile, cook bacon in a medium skillet until crisp. Add onions, celery, and garlic; cook until vegetables are tender, about 5 to 8 minutes. Add to beans and continue to simmer, covered, 2 hours.

4 Remove 1 cup beans with a slotted spoon and transfer to a food processor or blender. Puree mixture until smooth then return to soup. Remove ham hocks and cool. Remove meat from bones; dicscard skin and bones. Dice meat and return to soup. Add parsley and simmer 30 minutes more. Stir in salt, pepper, and vinegar. Makes 6 servings.

PER SERVING		DAILY GOAL
Calories	366	2,000 (F), 2,500 (M)
Total Fat	5 g	60 g or less (F), 70 g or less (M)
Saturated fat	2 g	20 g or less (F), 23 g or less (M)
Cholesterol	20 mg	300 mg or less
Sodium	960 mg	2,400 mg or less
Carbohydrates	56 g	250 g or more
Protein	25 g	55 g to 90 g

NOTES

60

SMOKY BLACK
BEAN SOUP

Smoked ham hocks provide the backbone of flavor in this classic bean soup. Red pepper flakes heat things up—add as much as you please.

▼ *Low-fat*
▽ *Low-calorie*
Prep time: 45 minutes plus soaking
Cooking time: 1½ to 2 hours
○ *Degree of difficulty: easy*

1 **pound black beans**
  Water
1 **tablespoon vegetable oil**
2 **cups chopped onions**
1 **cup peeled, chopped carrots**
1 **cup chopped celery**
1 **tablespoon minced garlic**
2 **teaspoons cumin**
¼ **to ½ teaspoon red pepper flakes**
2 **cans (13¾ *or* 14½ ounces each)**
  chicken broth *or* 3½ cups Rich
  Chicken Stock (recipe, page 29)
½ **bay leaf**
¼ **teaspoon thyme**

1 **pound smoked ham hocks**
1 **can (14½ *or* 16 ounces) tomatoes,**
  chopped, liquid reserved
1½ **teaspoons salt**
  Lemon slices, for garnish

1 Rinse beans and pick over for small stones and shriveled beans. In a large bowl, cover beans with 2 inches water and soak overnight. (To quick-soak: Combine beans with water to cover by 2 inches in a large saucepan and bring to a boil; boil 2 minutes. Cover and let stand 1 hour.) Drain in a colander; set aside.

2 Heat oil in a large Dutch oven over medium heat. Add onions, carrots, and celery. Cook, stirring occasionally, until tender, 10 minutes. Add garlic, cumin, and pepper flakes and cook 30 seconds. Stir in beans, broth, 4 cups water, bay leaf, thyme, and ham hocks; bring to a boil. Reduce heat, cover, and simmer 30 minutes. Stir in tomatoes with liquid. Cover and simmer until beans are very tender, 1 to 1½ hours more. Stir in salt.

3 Remove ham hock. When cool enough to handle, cut meat from bones; discard skin and bones and bay leaf. Dice meat and return to soup. With a potato masher, mash soup to thicken. Spoon into soup bowls and top each with a lemon slice. Makes 8 servings.

PER SERVING		DAILY GOAL
Calories	293	2,000 (F), 2,500 (M)
Total Fat	6 g	60 g or less (F), 70 g or less (M)
Saturated fat	2 g	20 g or less (F), 23 g or less (M)
Cholesterol	11 mg	300 mg or less
Sodium	1,280 mg	2,400 mg or less
Carbohydrates	45 g	250 g or more
Protein	18 g	55 g to 90 g

NOTES

_____

_____

_____

_____

_____

_____

_____

_____

_____

_____

_____

SPLIT PEA SOUP WITH GARLIC CROUTONS

Here's a great soup to have in your freezer when a dose of warmth is needed. You can use green or yellow split peas.

Prep time: 30 minutes
Cooking time: 1 hour
○ *Degree of difficulty: easy*

1 tablespoon vegetable oil
2 cups peeled, chopped carrots
1 cup chopped onions
1 cup chopped celery
8 ounces baked ham, diced
1 tablespoon minced garlic
¼ teaspoon cloves
¼ teaspoon ground red pepper
1 pound green split peas, rinsed and picked over
2 cans (13¾ *or* 14½ ounces each) chicken broth *or* 3½ cups Rich Chicken Stock (recipe, page 29)
10 cups water
1 bay leaf
1 teaspoon salt
½ teaspoon freshly ground pepper

Garlic Croutons
3 tablespoons olive oil
1 teaspoon minced garlic
½ teaspoon salt
½ teaspoon freshly ground pepper
6 slices firm white bread, cubed

1 Heat oil in a large Dutch oven over medium-high heat. Add carrots, onions, celery, and ham. Cook, stirring, until vegetables are softened, 10 minutes. Stir in garlic, cloves, and red pepper and cook 30 seconds. Add split peas, broth, water, bay leaf, salt, and pepper; bring to a boil. Reduce heat and simmer uncovered, stirring occasionally, until peas are tender, 1 hour.

2 Remove bay leaf. Puree 6 cups soup in blender in 2 batches and return to Dutch oven. Spoon soup into bowls and serve with Garlic Croutons. Makes 8 servings.

Garlic Croutons: Preheat oven to 425°F. Combine oil, garlic, salt, and pepper in a large bowl. Add bread and toss to coat. Spread on a 15½x10½-inch jelly-roll pan and bake 10 minutes or until golden, stirring halfway through. Cool.

PER SERVING WITH CROUTONS		DAILY GOAL
Calories	395	2,000 (F), 2,500 (M)
Total Fat	12 g	60 g or less (F), 70 g or less (M)
Saturated fat	2 g	20 g or less (F), 23 g or less (M)
Cholesterol	17 mg	300 mg or less
Sodium	1,482 mg	2,400 mg or less
Carbohydrates	50 g	250 g or more
Protein	23 g	55 g to 90 g

NOTES

_____
_____
_____
_____
_____
_____
_____
_____
_____
_____
_____
_____
_____
_____
_____

SAVORY MUSHROOM-BARLEY SOUP

We've used chuck steak to give this grain and vegetable soup its extra-rich flavor.

Prep time: 25 minutes
Cooking time: 2 hours
○ *Degree of difficulty: easy*

1½ **pounds bone-in beef chuck, cut into ¾-inch cubes**
     Salt
     Freshly ground pepper
2 **tablespoons vegetable oil, divided**
2 **cups finely chopped onions**
1 **cup peeled, diced carrots**
½ **cup finely chopped celery**
1 **pound fresh mushrooms, sliced**
1 **teaspoon minced garlic**
¼ **teaspoon thyme**
1 **can (13¾ or 14½ ounces) beef broth or 1¾ cups Hearty Beef Stock (recipe, page 30)**
1 **can (13¾ or 14½ ounces) chicken broth or 1¾ cups Rich Chicken Stock (recipe, page 29)**
   Water
½ **cup pearl barley**
3 **tablespoons chopped fresh parsley**

1 Sprinkle beef with salt and pepper. Heat 1 tablespoon of the oil in a large Dutch oven over medium-high heat. Brown beef and bone in 2 batches and transfer to a plate. Heat remaining 1 tablespoon oil in same pot. Add onions, carrots, and celery. Cover and cook, stirring occasionally, until vegetables are tender, 5 minutes. Stir in mushrooms, garlic, and thyme; cook, covered, 3 minutes more.

2 Meanwhile, combine beef and chicken broths with enough water to equal 6 cups. Stir into pot with barley, ¾ teaspoon salt and ½ teaspoon pepper; bring to a boil. Reduce heat and simmer covered until beef is tender, 1½ hours. Remove meat from bone and discard bone. Add meat to pot and stir in parsley. Makes 6 servings.

PER SERVING		DAILY GOAL
Calories	398	2,000 (F), 2,500 (M)
Total Fat	24 g	60 g or less (F), 70 g or less (M)
Saturated fat	8 g	20 g or less (F), 23 g or less (M)
Cholesterol	66 mg	300 mg or less
Sodium	1,008 mg	2,400 mg or less
Carbohydrates	24 g	250 g or more
Protein	21 g	55 g to 90 g

SPEEDY TORTELLINI SOUP

This pasta and vegetable soup is spiced just right thanks to a dollop of prepared pesto.

▽ *Low-calorie*
  Prep time: 15 minutes
  Cooking time: 15 minutes
○ *Degree of difficulty: easy*

1 tablespoon olive oil
1 medium onion, chopped
½ cup diced carrots
2 cans (13¾ *or* 14½ ounces each) chicken broth *or* 3½ cups Rich Chicken Stock (recipe, page 29)
1 package (9 ounces) cheese tortellini
1 cup escarole *or* spinach
½ cup frozen peas
2 tablespoons freshly grated Parmesan cheese
2 tablespoons prepared pesto
   Salt and freshly ground pepper

1 Heat oil in a large saucepan over medium heat. Add onion and carrots. Cook, stirring frequently, until vegetables are softened, 3 minutes. Add chicken broth and bring to a boil.

2 Reduce heat and stir in tortellini. Simmer until tortellini are cooked, 5 to 8 minutes. Stir in escarole, peas, cheese, pesto, and salt and pepper to taste. Simmer 1 minute more or until escarole is just tender. Makes 4 servings.

PER SERVING		DAILY GOAL
Calories	340	2,000 (F), 2,500 (M)
Total Fat	13 g	60 g or less (F), 70 g or less (M)
Saturated fat	2 g	20 g or less (F), 23 g or less (M)
Cholesterol	38 mg	300 mg or less
Sodium	1,439 mg	2,400 mg or less
Carbohydrates	40 g	250 g or more
Protein	16 g	55 g to 90 g

65

SIMPLY-FOR-
COMFORT STEWS

What could be more comforting when temperatures plunge than a hearty, old-fashioned stew? Here's a collection of slow-simmering favorites we've made easier than ever. One pot is all you'll need to prepare your favorite Beef Carbonnade with dark beer, classic Irish Stew, or Hungarian Pork Goulash— you don't even have to brown the meat! And, you'll love our Pressure-Cooker Beef Stew that's ready to savor in just minutes.

PORK STEW
WITH FENNEL

A little fennel seed goes a long way to flavor this lusty pork stew that's prepared with white wine and tomatoes.

▽ *Low-calorie*
Prep time: 25 minutes
Cooking time: 2½ hours
○ *Degree of difficulty: easy*

2 **teaspoons minced garlic**
1½ **teaspoons salt**
2 **pounds boneless pork loin, cut into**
      1½-inch cubes
3 **cups finely chopped onions**
½ **teaspoon freshly ground pepper**
¼ **teaspoon fennel seed**
1 **can (14½ *or* 16 ounces) tomatoes,**
      chopped and liquid reserved
3 **cups celery, cut into 1-inch pieces**
½ **cup white wine**
1 **package (10 ounces) frozen peas**

1 Preheat oven to 325°F. With the flat side of a large knife, crush garlic with salt to form a paste. Combine garlic paste with pork, onions, pepper, and fennel seed in a large, heavy Dutch oven. Cover and roast 1½ hours.

2 Stir in tomatoes with liquid, celery, white wine, and peas. Cover and cook 1 hour more or until pork is tender. Stir in peas. Makes 6 servings.

PER SERVING		DAILY GOAL
Calories	333	2,000 (F), 2,500 (M)
Total Fat	12 g	60 g or less (F), 70 g or less (M)
Saturated fat	4 g	20 g or less (F), 23 g or less (M)
Cholesterol	96 mg	300 mg or less
Sodium	865 mg	2,400 mg or less
Carbohydrates	17 g	250 g or more
Protein	37 g	55 g to 90 g

NOTES

68

PORK AND GREEN CHILI STEW

This stew boasts a double dose of fresh chili flavor from roasted poblanos and minced jalapeños. If it's a milder flavor you seek, substitute sweet green peppers for the poblanos.

Prep time: 35 minutes
Cooking time: 2 hours 20 minutes
Degree of difficulty: easy

4 **poblano chilies *or* 2 green peppers**
1 **tablespoon minced garlic**
 Salt
1½ **pounds trimmed, boneless, lean pork shoulder, cut into 1½-inch cubes**
3 **cups finely chopped onions**
¼ **cup minced jalapeño peppers**
½ **teaspoon oregano**
1½ **pounds red new potatoes, quartered**
½ **cup chopped fresh cilantro**
3 **zucchini, halved lengthwise and sliced ½ inch thick**
1 **package (10 ounces) frozen whole-kernel corn, thawed**
 Lime wedges, for garnish

1 Preheat broiler. Roast poblanos 5 inches from heat 25 minutes, turning every 5 minutes, or until skin is charred. Cover and cool. Peel the skin from the chilies with a small sharp knife; discard skin and seeds and coarsely chop chilies.

2 Preheat oven to 325°F. With the flat side of a large knife, crush garlic with salt to form a paste. Combine garlic paste with poblanos, pork, onions, jalapeños, and oregano in a large, heavy Dutch oven. Cover and roast 1½ hours.

3 Stir in potatoes and chopped cilantro. Cover and cook 30 minutes. Add zucchini, corn, and ½ teaspoon salt and cook 20 minutes more or until pork and vegetables are tender. Garnish with lime wedges. Makes 6 servings.

PER SERVING		DAILY GOAL
Calories	375	2,000 (F), 2,500 (M)
Total Fat	10 g	60 g or less (F), 70 g or less (M)
Saturated fat	3 g	20 g or less (F), 23 g or less (M)
Cholesterol	77 mg	300 mg or less
Sodium	657 mg	2,400 mg or less
Carbohydrates	47 g	250 g or more
Protein	28 g	55 g to 90 g

NOTES

HUNGARIAN PORK GOULASH

The key ingredient to this classic stew is paprika. The sweet, imported variety is recommended for a guaranteed rich and mellow flavor. *Also pictured on page 66.*

▽ *Low-calorie*
   Prep time: 25 minutes
   Cooking time: 2½ to 3 hours
○ *Degree of difficulty: easy*

  2 **teaspoons minced garlic**
  2 **teaspoons salt**
  2 **pounds trimmed, boneless, lean pork shoulder, cut into 1½-inch cubes**
1½ **cups chopped onions**
  3 **tablespoons tomato paste**
  2 **tablespoons paprika**
  ½ **teaspoon freshly ground pepper**
  2 **cups sauerkraut, rinsed and drained**
  1 **teaspoon caraway seed**
  ½ **cup sour cream**
     Cooked egg noodles

1 Preheat oven to 325°F. With the flat side of a large knife, crush garlic with salt to form a paste. Combine garlic paste with pork, onions, tomato paste, paprika, and pepper in a large, heavy Dutch oven. Cover and roast 1½ hours.

2 Stir in sauerkraut and caraway. Cover and cook 45 to 60 minutes more or until pork is very tender. Remove from heat and stir in sour cream. Serve with cooked egg noodles. Makes 6 servings.

PER SERVING
WITHOUT NOODLES

		DAILY GOAL
Calories	314	2,000 (F), 2,500 (M)
Total Fat	16 g	60 g or less (F), 70 g or less (M)
Saturated fat	7 g	20 g or less (F), 23 g or less (M)
Cholesterol	110 mg	300 mg or less
Sodium	1,107 mg	2,400 mg or less
Carbohydrates	9 g	250 g or more
Protein	31 g	55 g to 90 g

71

COUNTRY FRENCH PORK AND WHITE BEAN STEW

We love this stew with a spicy garlic sausage, but kielbasa is tasty, too. If you're preparing the stew ahead, cover the pot and refrigerate up to 24 hours, then reheat in a 350°F oven for 1 hour.

Prep time: 20 minutes plus soaking
Cooking time: 2 hours 10 minutes
Degree of difficulty: easy

- 1 **pound dried Great Northern beans**
- 1 **tablespoon vegetable oil**
- 2 **pounds boneless pork shoulder, cut into 1½-inch cubes**
  Salt
  Freshly ground pepper
- 2 **cups chopped onions**
- 1 **tablespoon minced garlic**
- 8 **ounces garlic sausage *or* kielbasa (halved lengthwise if thick), sliced ½ inch thick**
- 2 **cans (13¾ *or* 14½ ounces each) *or* 3½ cups Rich Chicken Stock (recipe, page 29)**
- ½ **cup water**
- ½ **bay leaf**
- ½ **teaspoon thyme**
- 2 **tablespoons tomato paste**
- ¼ **cup chopped fresh parsley**

1 Rinse beans and pick over for small stones and shriveled beans. In a large bowl, cover beans with 2 inches water and soak overnight. (To quick-soak: Combine beans with water to cover by 2 inches in a large saucepan and bring to a boil; boil 2 minutes. Cover and let stand 1 hour.) Drain in a colander; set aside.

2 Preheat oven to 350°F. Heat oil in a large Dutch oven over high heat. Sprinkle 1 pound of the pork with salt and pepper; add to Dutch oven and brown well on all sides, 5 minutes. Transfer pork to a bowl with a slotted spoon. Repeat process with remaining 1 pound pork.

3 Reduce heat to medium. Add onions to Dutch oven and cook, stirring occasionally, until tender, 5 minutes. Stir in garlic and cook until fragrant, 30 seconds. Return pork to pot and add beans, sausage, broth, water, bay leaf, thyme, and ½ teaspoon pepper; bring to a boil. Cover and transfer to the oven. Bake 1 hour.

4 Combine wine and tomato paste in a small bowl and stir into the stew. Cover and bake 1 hour more. Sprinkle with parsley. Makes 10 servings.

PER SERVING		DAILY GOAL
Calories	406	2,000 (F), 2,500 (M)
Total Fat	15 g	60 g or less (F), 70 g or less (M)
Saturated fat	6 g	20 g or less (F), 23 g or less (M)
Cholesterol	76 mg	300 mg or less
Sodium	756 mg	2,400 mg or less
Carbohydrates	32 g	250 g or more
Protein	32 g	55 g to 90 g

NOTES

FRAGRANT INDIAN BEEF STEW

We've come up with a special curry blend for this aromatic stew, packed with spices and veggies. Try it with lamb, too.

Prep time: 40 minutes
Cooking time: 1 hour 40 minutes
○ *Degree of difficulty: easy*

2   **pounds boneless beef round, cut into 1-inch cubes**
2   **tablespoons vegetable oil**
2   **tablespoons butter *or* margarine**
4   **cups finely chopped onions (about 2 pounds)**
4   **large garlic cloves, minced**
1   **tablespoon minced fresh ginger**
1   **tablespoon minced jalapeño peppers**
2   **tablespoons ground coriander**
1   **tablespoon cumin**
1   **teaspoon turmeric**
1½ **teaspoons salt**
½   **teaspoon freshly ground pepper**
1   **can (14½ *or* 16 ounces) tomatoes, coarsely chopped and liquid reserved**

Water
2   **cups cauliflower florets**
8   **ounces carrots, peeled and diced**
1   **pound potatoes, peeled and diced**
1   **cup frozen peas**

1 Pat beef dry on paper towels. Heat oil in a large Dutch oven over high heat. Add half the beef and brown well on all sides. Transfer with a slotted spoon to a bowl. Repeat with remaining beef and set aside. Drain oil.

2 Preheat oven to 350°F. Melt butter in Dutch oven over medium heat. Add onions, garlic, ginger, and jalapeño. Cook, stirring occasionally, until lightly browned, about 10 to 15 minutes. Add coriander, cumin, turmeric, salt, and pepper and cook 2 minutes. Add beef, tomatoes with liquid, and 2 cups water; bring to a boil. Cover and bake 1½ hours or until beef is tender.

3 Meanwhile, bring 1½ quarts of salted water to a boil in a large saucepan. Add cauliflower and simmer until tender, 5 to 7 minutes. With a slotted spoon, transfer to a medium bowl. Cook carrots in the same saucepan until tender, 5 to 7 minutes, and then add to the cauliflower. Cover potatoes with hot water in a small saucepan and bring to a boil. Cook until tender, 10 to 15 minutes. Drain and add to vegetables.

4 Add vegetables and peas to Dutch oven. Cover and bake until heated through, about 10 minutes. (Can be made ahead. Cool. Cover and refrigerate up to 3 days. Heat in 350°F. oven 20 minutes.) Makes 8 servings.

PER SERVING		DAILY GOAL
Calories	406	2,000 (F), 2,500 (M)
Total Fat	21 g	60 g or less (F), 70 g or less (M)
Saturated fat	8 g	20 g or less (F), 23 g or less (M)
Cholesterol	79 mg	300 mg or less
Sodium	631 mg	2,400 mg or less
Carbohydrates	28 g	250 g or more
Protein	28 g	55 g to 90 g

NOTES

OLD-FASHIONED BEEF STEW

We've trimmed the fat and calories in this savory classic by slow-roasting all the stew ingredients in a heavy Dutch oven. It tastes even better when reheated! *Also pictured on the cover.*

▼　*Low-fat*
▽　*Low-calorie*
　　Prep time: 25 minutes
　　Cooking time: 2½ to 3 hours
○　*Degree of difficulty: easy*

- 2　**teaspoons minced garlic**
- 1½　**teaspoons salt**
- 2　**pounds round steak, trimmed of all fat and cut into 1-inch cubes**
- 3　**cups finely chopped onions**
- ½　**teaspoon thyme**
- ½　**teaspoon freshly ground pepper**
- 2　**tablespoons tomato paste**
- 1　**pound carrots, peeled and cut into 1-inch pieces**
- 3　**cups celery, cut into 1-inch pieces**
- 1　**pound fresh mushrooms, trimmed**
- 1　**pound small white onions, peeled**

1 Preheat oven to 325°F. With the flat side of a large knife, crush the garlic with salt to form a paste. Combine the garlic paste with beef, onions, thyme, and pepper in a large, heavy Dutch oven. Cover and roast 1½ hours.

2 Stir in tomato paste, carrots, celery, mushrooms, and onions. Cover and cook until beef and vegetables are tender, 1 to 1½ hours more. Makes 6 servings.

PER SERVING		DAILY GOAL
Calories	333	2,000 (F), 2,500 (M)
Total Fat	8 g	60 g or less (F), 70 g or less (M)
Saturated fat	3 g	20 g or less (F), 23 g or less (M)
Cholesterol	88 mg	300 mg or less
Sodium	768 mg	2,400 mg or less
Carbohydrates	26 g	250 g or more
Protein	38 g	55 g to 90 g

NOTES

74

RUTABAGA-BEEF STEW

Like turnips, rutabagas are at their peak July through April. High in calcium and vitamins, this sweet root vegetable is delicious combined with a touch of orange in this stew.

▽ *Low-calorie*
   Prep time: 25 minutes
   Cooking time: 1 hour 45 minutes
○ *Degree of difficulty: easy*

¼ **cup all-purpose flour**
¾ **teaspoon rosemary, crushed**
¼ **teaspoon freshly ground pepper**
1½ **pounds lean, boneless beef chuck, cut into 1½ inch pieces**
2 **tablespoons vegetable oil, divided**
1 **medium onion, chopped**
1 **cup orange juice**
½ **cup canned beef broth *or* Hearty Beef Stock (recipe, page 30)**
1½ **pounds rutabaga, peeled and cut into 1-inch pieces**
3 **medium potatoes, peeled and cut into 1-inch pieces**
   Salt

1 Combine flour, rosemary, and pepper in a large bowl. Add beef, tossing to coat. Heat 1 tablespoon of the oil in a large Dutch oven over medium-high heat. Add half the beef and the onions to the pot; brown well on all sides. Transfer beef with a slotted spoon to a plate. Repeat with remaining beef, adding remaining oil as needed. Add orange juice and beef broth, stirring to scrape up browned bits from the bottom of pan. Return beef to pot; bring to a boil. Reduce heat to low; cover and simmer 1 hour.

2 Add rutabaga and potatoes to pot. Cover and simmer until meat and vegetables are tender, 45 minutes more. (Add additional beef broth if stew becomes too dry.) Season with salt if desired. Makes 6 servings.

PER SERVING		DAILY GOAL
Calories	345	2,000 (F), 2,500 (M)
Total Fat	13 g	60 g or less (F), 70 g or less (M)
Saturated fat	4 g	20 g or less (F), 23 g or less (M)
Cholesterol	74 mg	300 mg or less
Sodium	199 mg	2,400 mg or less
Carbohydrates	30 g	250 g or more
Protein	26 g	55 g to 90 g

NOTES

BEEF CARBONNADE

This national dish from Belgium is a thick and hearty brew of beef, onions, brown sugar, and dark beer.

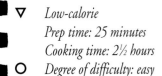

▽ *Low-calorie*
   Prep time: 25 minutes
   Cooking time: 2½ hours
O *Degree of difficulty: easy*

2 **teaspoons minced garlic**
1 **teaspoon salt**
2 **pounds lean, boneless beef chuck, cut into 1½-inch cubes**
2 **tablespoons flour**
1½ **cups chopped onions**
1 **tablespoon Dijon mustard**
1 **tablespoon cider vinegar**
1 **teaspoon packed brown sugar**
½ **teaspoon freshly ground pepper**
½ **teaspoon thyme**
½ **teaspoon marjoram**
1 **bottle (12 ounces) dark beer**
1½ **cups sliced onions**
   Boiled potatoes

1 Preheat oven to 325°F. With the flat side of a large knife, crush garlic with salt to form a paste.

2 Place the beef in a large, heavy Dutch oven; sprinkle with flour and toss to coat. Add the garlic paste, chopped onions, mustard, vinegar, brown sugar, pepper, thyme, and marjoram. Stir to combine. Cover and roast 1 hour.

3 Bring beer to a boil in a small saucepan. Add the beer and sliced onions to pot. Cover and cook 1 hour, then uncover and cook 30 minutes more. Serve with boiled potatoes. Makes 6 servings.

PER SERVING		DAILY GOAL
Calories	284	2,000 (F), 2,500 (M)
Total Fat	11 g	60 g or less (F), 70 g or less (M)
Saturated fat	4 g	20 g or less (F), 23 g or less (M)
Cholesterol	98 mg	300 mg or less
Sodium	564 mg	2,400 mg or less
Carbohydrates	13 g	250 g or more
Protein	31 g	55 g to 90 g

PRESSURE-COOKER BEEF STEW

The old pressure cooker is back in style, and it's easy to see why. This slow-cooking Burgundy-style stew is tender and delicious in one-fourth of the time it would normally take.

Prep time: 25 minutes plus marinating and standing
Cooking time: 25 minutes
○ *Degree of difficulty: easy*

1   cup red wine
1¼ teaspoons salt
½   teaspoon freshly ground pepper
½   teaspoon thyme
1   bay leaf
2   pounds lean, boneless beef chuck, cut into 1-inch cubes
3   tablespoons butter *or* margarine
1   cup chopped onions
3   tablespoons all-purpose flour
8   ounces small fresh mushrooms
18 small white onions, peeled
6   carrots, peeled and cut into 1-inch pieces
8   ounces wide egg noodles, cooked according to package directions

1   For marinade, combine wine, salt, pepper, thyme, and bay leaf in a medium glass bowl. Stir in beef. Cover and refrigerate overnight. Transfer meat with a slotted spoon to paper towels to drain. Reserve marinade.

2   Melt butter in a 4-quart pressure-cooker over high heat. Add half the beef and brown well on all sides, about 4 minutes. Remove beef and set aside. Repeat with remaining beef; remove and set aside. Add onions and cook until tender, 10 minutes. Stir in flour and cook, stirring 1 minute. Stir in marinade; bring to a boil, stirring to scrape up browned bits. Return beef to the pot.

3   Lock lid in place and set control at 15. Place over high heat with pressure regulator on vent pipe. When pressure regulator starts to rock, reduce heat to medium to maintain pressure and cook 13 minutes. Remove from heat and let pressure drop, about 10 minutes.

4   Open cooker, add the mushrooms, onions, and carrots. Cover and set control to 15. Place over high heat with pressure regulator on vent pipe. When pressure regulator starts to rock, reduce heat to medium and cook 1 minute. Remove from heat and let pressure drop, about 10 minutes. Remove bay leaf. Serve beef over noodles. Makes 6 servings.

PER SERVING		DAILY GOAL
Calories	502	2,000 (F), 2,500 (M)
Total Fat	19 g	60 g or less (F), 70 g or less (M)
Saturated fat	8 g	20 g or less (F), 23 g or less (M)
Cholesterol	150 mg	300 mg or less
Sodium	673 mg	2,400 mg or less
Carbohydrates	45 g	250 g or more
Protein	37 g	55 g to 90 g

NOTES

MEDITERRANEAN BEEF AND OKRA STEW

This stew is also delicious prepared with boneless leg of lamb.

▽ *Low-calorie*
Prep time: 20 minutes
Cooking time: 2 to 2½ hours
○ *Degree of difficulty: easy*

2 **teaspoons minced garlic**
2 **teaspoons salt**
2 **pounds lean beef chuck** *or*
   boneless leg of lamb, cut into
   1½-inch cubes
1½ **cups chopped onions**
½ **teaspoon freshly ground pepper**
¼ **teaspoon ground red pepper**
1 **pound fresh okra** *or* **2 packages**
   (10 ounces each) frozen whole
   okra, cut in half
1 **can (14½ or 16 ounces) tomatoes,**
   chopped and liquid reserved

1 Preheat oven to 325°F. With the flat side of a large knife, crush garlic with salt to form a paste. Combine garlic paste with meat, onions, and red and black peppers in a large, heavy Dutch oven. Cover and roast 1 hour.

2 Stir in okra and tomatoes with liquid. Cover and cook until meat is very tender, 1 to 1½ hours more. Makes 6 servings.

PER SERVING WITH BEEF		DAILY GOAL
Calories	286	2,000 (F), 2,500 (M)
Total Fat	12 g	60 g or less (F), 70 g or less (M)
Saturated fat	4 g	20 g or less (F), 23 g or less (M)
Cholesterol	98 mg	300 mg or less
Sodium	975 mg	2,400 mg or less
Carbohydrates	13 g	250 g or more
Protein	32 g	55 g to 90 g

PER SERVING WITH LAMB		DAILY GOAL
Calories	254	2,000 (F), 2,500 (M)
Total Fat	7 g	60 g or less (F), 70 g or less (M)
Saturated fat	2 g	20 g or less (F), 23 g or less (M)
Cholesterol	97 mg	300 mg or less
Sodium	952 mg	2,400 mg or less
Carbohydrates	13 g	250 g or more
Protein	34 g	55 g to 90 g

NOTES

79

CHICKEN AND SAUSAGE GUMBO

This lusty stew from New Orleans gets its unique flavor from roux, flour and oil slowly cooked to a rich, dark brown.

Prep time: 1 hour
Cooking time: 1 hour
Degree of difficulty: easy

1 **whole chicken (3 pounds), quartered**
3 **tablespoons vegetable oil**
⅓ **cup all-purpose flour**
2 **cups chopped onions**
¾ **cup chopped green pepper**
½ **cup chopped celery**
1 **teaspoon minced garlic**
¾ **teaspoon salt**
¼ **teaspoon thyme**
⅛ **teaspoon ground red pepper (optional)**
8 **ounces andouille *or* smoked garlic sausage, halved lengthwise and sliced ¼ inch thick**
1 **package (10 ounces) frozen cut okra, thawed**
 Cooked rice

1 Place chicken in a deep skillet with enough cold water to cover; bring to a boil and cook 2 minutes. Remove from heat; cover and let stand 40 minutes. Strain broth into a large bowl and reserve. Remove chicken. When cool enough to handle, remove meat and tear into large pieces, discarding skin and bones.

2 Heat oil in a large Dutch oven over medium heat. Add flour and cook, stirring constantly, until mixture becomes a nutty brown color, 15 minutes. Add onions, pepper, and celery. Cook, stirring occasionally, until vegetables are just tender, about 10 minutes. Add garlic and cook 30 seconds more.

3 Gradually whisk in 4 cups reserved chicken broth. (Cool remaining broth. Cover and freeze for another use.) Add chicken meat, salt, thyme, and red pepper; bring to a boil and simmer 10 minutes. Add sausage and okra; continue to cook until okra is tender, 12 to 15 minutes more. Serve over rice. Makes 6 servings.

PER SERVING		DAILY GOAL
Calories	372	2,000 (F), 2,500 (M)
Total Fat	21 g	60 g or less (F), 70 g or less (M)
Saturated fat	5 g	20 g or less (F), 23 g or less (M)
Cholesterol	102 mg	300 mg or less
Sodium	778 mg	2,400 mg or less
Carbohydrates	15 g	250 g or more
Protein	31 g	55 g to 90 g

NOTES

81

ONE-POT BRUNSWICK STEW

We've cut the fat and calories from this classic chicken stew and kept all the fixings in one pot.

▼ *Low-fat*
▽ *Low-calorie*
    Prep time: 30 minutes plus cooling
    Cooking time: 1½ hours
○ *Degree of difficulty: easy*

1 **roasting chicken (4 to 5 pounds), skinned and cut up**
2 **cups water**
2 **cans (13¾ *or* 14½ ounces each) chicken broth *or* Rich Chicken Stock, (recipe, page 29)**
2 **cups chopped celery**
2 **medium onions, chopped**
1 **cup chopped green pepper**
1 **garlic clove, minced**
¼ **cup chopped fresh parsley**
1 **teaspoon thyme**
3 **tablespoons Worcestershire sauce**
1 **teaspoon hot pepper sauce**

1 **can (28 ounces) chopped tomatoes, liquid reserved, *or* 4 ripe tomatoes, peeled and chopped**
1 **teaspoon salt**
½ **teaspoon freshly ground pepper**
1 **bag (16 ounces) frozen whole-kernel corn**
1 **package (10 ounces) frozen lima beans**
1 **package (10 ounces) frozen cut okra**

1 Combine chicken, water, chicken broth, celery, onions, green pepper, garlic, parsley, thyme, Worcestershire sauce, hot pepper sauce, tomatoes with liquid, salt, and pepper; bring to a boil. Reduce heat; cover and simmer 1 hour.

2 Remove chicken with a slotted spoon to a platter and cool. Remove meat from bones; tear into large pieces and return to Dutch oven. Discard skin and bones. Add corn, lima beans, and okra. Return to a simmer and cook 30 minutes. Makes 8 servings.

PER SERVING		DAILY GOAL
Calories	311	2,000 (F), 2,500 (M)
Total Fat	6 g	60 g or less (F), 70 g or less (M)
Saturated fat	1 g	20 g or less (F), 23 g or less (M)
Cholesterol	86 mg	300 mg or less
Sodium	1,173 mg	2,400 mg or less
Carbohydrates	33 g	250 g or more
Protein	34 g	55 g to 90 g

NOTES

SPICY LAMB AND LENTIL STEW

Budget cuts like lamb shoulder are ideal in this stew, where the lamb is simmered in a spicy broth with lentils.

Prep time: 20 minutes
Cooking time: 1½ hours
○ *Degree of difficulty: easy*

4 tablespoons olive oil, divided
2 pounds lean, boneless lamb shoulder, cut into 1-inch cubes
1¾ cups diced onions
2 tablespoons paprika
2 tablespoons minced garlic
2 teaspoons nutmeg
1 can (28 ounces) tomatoes, drained and chopped
2 cans (13¾ or 14½ ounces each) beef broth plus enough water to equal 4 cups or 4 cups Hearty Beef Stock (recipe, page 30)
½ teaspoon salt
⅛ teaspoon ground red pepper
2 cups dried lentils, rinsed and picked over
¼ cup fresh lemon juice
½ cup pitted and chopped Niçoise or Kalamata olives
2 tablespoons minced fresh mint

1 Heat 2 tablespoons of the oil in a large Dutch oven over medium-high heat. Add half the lamb and cook until browned well on all sides, about 5 minutes. Remove meat with a slotted spoon to a plate and repeat with the remaining oil and lamb. Set lamb aside.

2 Add onions to Dutch oven and cook until softened, 5 minutes. Return lamb to pot and stir in paprika, garlic, and nutmeg. Cook, stirring, 2 minutes more. Add tomatoes, broth, salt, and red pepper; bring to a boil. Reduce heat and simmer covered until meat is almost tender, stirring occasionally, 1 hour.

3 Add lentils to pot and cook uncovered until meat and lentils are tender, about 30 minutes more. Just before serving, stir in lemon juice and top with olives and mint. Makes 8 servings.

PER SERVING		DAILY GOAL
Calories	451	2,000 (F), 2,500 (M)
Total Fat	17 g	60 g or less (F), 70 g or less (M)
Saturated fat	4 g	20 g or less (F), 23 g or less (M)
Cholesterol	75 mg	300 mg or less
Sodium	921 mg	2,400 mg or less
Carbohydrates	38 g	250 g or more
Protein	38 g	55 g to 90 g

NOTES

83

IRISH STEW

Nothing could be simpler. Layers of potatoes, onions, and lamb are arranged and roasted in one pot. Begin preparation a day before serving to allow all the flavors to develop.

Prep time: 25 minutes plus chilling
Cooking time: 2½ to 3 hours
○ *Degree of difficulty: easy*

2½ **pounds potatoes, peeled and sliced**
1½ **pounds onions, sliced ¼ inch thick**
3   **pounds lean lamb shoulder, cubed**
2   **teaspoons salt**
½   **teaspoon freshly ground pepper**
½   **teaspoon thyme**
2   **cups water**
1   **tablespoon Worcestershire sauce**
1   **bay leaf**
¼   **cup chopped fresh parsley**

1 Preheat oven to 325°F. Layer one-third of the potatoes, then half the onions, and the lamb in a large, heavy Dutch oven. Combine salt, pepper, and thyme in a cup and sprinkle half of the mixture over top of the meat. Repeat layering with remaining onions and lamb, top with remaining potatoes and sprinkle with remaining salt and pepper mixture. Add water, Worcestershire sauce, and bay leaf, then sprinkle with parsley; bring to a boil over medium heat. Cover and bake until meat is tender, 1½ to 2 hours more. Cool to room temperature. Cover and refrigerate overnight.

2 Spoon fat from top of stew and discard. Bake uncovered in a 325°F. oven until hot and bubbly, 1 hour. Remove bay leaf. Makes 8 servings.

PER SERVING		DAILY GOAL
Calories	365	2,000 (F), 2,500 (M)
Total Fat	12 g	60 g or less (F), 70 g or less (M)
Saturated fat	4 g	20 g or less (F), 23 g or less (M)
Cholesterol	112 mg	300 mg or less
Sodium	670 mg	2,400 mg or less
Carbohydrates	27 g	250 g or more
Protein	37 g	55 g to 90 g

ONE-POT ROASTING: TIPS FOR OUR EASIEST STEWS

Because you can simply throw all the ingredients into a pot and roast, our one-step stews are truly something special. They're lower in fat, and moist and tender without excess liquid. Here are some tips for stew perfection:

• **It's all in the pot.** The key to successful one-pot roasting is to start with a heavy Dutch oven with a tight-fitting lid. Your Dutch oven or heavy metal casserole should be large, and should be able to go from stove-top to oven. It should be made of cast iron, cast aluminum, or heavy stainless steel.

• **Form a tight seal.** If your lid does not fit securely on your Dutch oven or casserole, first wrap the top of the Dutch oven securely with a sheet of foil then place the lid on top.

MOROCCAN LAMB STEW

Fragrant with cumin, ginger, and cinnamon, this lamb stew comes to your table brimming with fresh vegetables and chick-peas. Couscous is a perfect accompaniment.

▼ *Low-fat*
▽ *Low-calorie*
  Prep time: 30 minutes
  Cooking time: 2 hours
○ *Degree of difficulty: easy*

- 2 teaspoons minced garlic
- 1½ teaspoons salt
- 2 pounds lean, boneless leg of lamb, cut into 1½-inch cubes
- 3 cups finely chopped onions
- 1 teaspoon cumin
- 1 teaspoon ginger
- ¼ teaspoon cinnamon
- ¼ teaspoon ground red pepper
- 1 pound carrots, cut into 1-inch pieces
- 1 pound peeled butternut squash, cut into 1-inch pieces
- 1 can (19 ounces) chick-peas (garbanzos), rinsed and drained
- ⅓ cup raisins
- 2 zucchini, cut into 1-inch pieces
- ½ cup chopped fresh cilantro

1 Preheat oven to 325°F. With the flat side of a large knife, crush garlic with salt to form a paste. Combine garlic paste with lamb, onions, cumin, ginger, cinnamon, and pepper in a large, heavy Dutch oven. Cover and roast 1 hour.

2 Stir in carrots, squash, chick-peas, and raisins. Cover and cook 30 minutes. Add zucchini and cook 30 minutes more or until lamb and vegetables are tender. Sprinkle with cilantro. Makes 6 servings.

PER SERVING		DAILY GOAL	
Calories	313	2,000 (F), 2,500 (M)	
Total Fat	8 g	60 g or less (F), 70 g or less (M)	
Saturated fat	3 g	20 g or less (F), 23 g or less (M)	
Cholesterol	79 mg	300 mg or less	
Sodium	627 mg	2,400 mg or less	
Carbohydrates	32 g	250 g or more	
Protein	29 g	55 g to 90 g	

85

QUICK OYSTER STEW

Fresh oysters, which are abundant in the fall months, are high in calcium and other minerals.

▽   *Low-calorie*
      Prep time: 10 minutes
      Cooking time: 7 to 8 minutes
○   *Degree of difficulty: easy*

1   **cup half-and-half cream**
1   **cup milk**
1   **can (8½ ounces) low-sodium cream-style corn**
¼   **teaspoon thyme**
      Pinch sage
      Pinch freshly ground pepper
12   **ounces fresh shucked oysters**
      Red pepper sauce

Combine half-and-half, milk, corn, thyme, sage, and pepper in a medium saucepan; bring to a boil. Reduce heat to medium-low. Add oysters; simmer until just cooked through and edges curl, 3 to 4 minutes. Add red pepper sauce to taste. Makes 4 servings.

PER SERVING		DAILY GOAL
Calories	218	2,000 (F), 2,500 (M)
Total Fat	11 g	60 g or less (F), 70 g or less (M)
Saturated fat	6 g	20 g or less (F), 23 g or less (M)
Cholesterol	78 mg	300 mg or less
Sodium	152 mg	2,400 mg or less
Carbohydrates	20 g	250 g or more
Protein	11 g	55 g to 90 g

NOTES

_____

86

PROVENÇAL SEAFOOD STEW

Use the microwave to cut the hassle and the fat in this fish stew which is ready in minutes. We called for cod here, but any firm-fleshed fish such as scrod, bass, or snapper can be substituted.

- Ⓜ *Microwave*
- ▼ *Low-fat*
- ▽ *Low-calorie*
  Prep time: 10 minutes
  Microwave time: 18 minutes
- ○ *Degree of difficulty: easy*

½ **cup thinly sliced onion**
2 **teaspoons olive oil**
½ **teaspoon minced garlic**
1 **3-inch strip orange peel**
1 **sprig fresh thyme**
1 **whole allspice**
1 **can (14½ *or* 16 ounces) tomatoes, liquid reserved**
1 **bottle (8 ounces) clam juice**
  Pinch red pepper flakes
  Salt
  Freshly ground pepper

12 **mussels, rinsed, cleaned, and scrubbed**
4 **jumbo shrimp, peeled and deveined**
8 **ounces cod fillet, cut into 4 pieces**
  Fresh thyme sprigs *or* basil leaves, for garnish

1 Combine onion, oil, garlic, orange peel, thyme, and allspice in a 2- or 3-quart glass, microwave-proof casserole with glass lid. Cover and microwave on high (100% power) 4 minutes. Press tomatoes with liquid through a food mill or sieve into casserole. Stir in clam juice and red pepper flakes. Cover and microwave on high (100% power) 7 minutes or until very hot, stirring once. Season with salt and pepper.

2 Arrange mussels around edge of casserole. Cover and microwave on high (100% power) 3 minutes or until mussels open. Transfer opened mussels to a medium bowl; cover and keep warm. Microwave casserole on high (100% power) 1 minute more or until more mussels open. (Discard any unopened mussels.) Transfer to the bowl and keep warm.

3 Place shrimp and cod in the hot broth. Microwave covered on high (100% power) 2½ to 3 minutes, or until fish just begins to flake and shrimp are pink. Spoon mussels, shrimp, and fillets in 4 large, warmed soup bowls. Ladle steaming broth evenly over seafood. Garnish with thyme sprig or basil and serve immediately. Makes 4 servings.

PER SERVING		DAILY GOAL
Calories	143	2,000 (F), 2,500 (M)
Total Fat	4 g	60 g or less (F), 70 g or less (M)
Saturated fat	1 g	20 g or less (F), 23 g or less (M)
Cholesterol	66 mg	300 mg or less
Sodium	425 mg	2,400 mg or less
Carbohydrates	8 g	250 g or more
Protein	19 g	55 g to 90 g

NOTES

_____

_____

_____

_____

_____

_____

_____

_____

VEGETABLE CURRY WITH CILANTRO YOGURT

This meatless stew gets its heartiness from lentils and lots of chunky veggies, and its spice from fresh ginger, jalapeño, and curry powder. The creamy Cilantro Yogurt sauce cools things down. Serve with plenty of rice or couscous.

▼ *Low-fat*
▽ *Low-calorie*
   Prep time: 20 minutes
   Cooking time: 70 minutes
○ *Degree of difficulty: easy*

4 teaspoons vegetable oil
1 cup chopped onions
1 tablespoon minced garlic
1 tablespoon minced jalapeño peppers (optional)
2 teaspoons minced fresh ginger
1 tablespoon cumin
1 teaspoon curry powder
1 cup dried lentils, picked over and rinsed
4 cups water

2 teaspoons salt
¼ teaspoon freshly ground pepper
1 small butternut squash, cut into ¾-inch cubes (about 2 cups)
1 large potato, peeled and cut into 1-inch dice
2 cups cauliflower florets
1 cup peeled, sliced carrots
1 cup frozen peas, thawed
¼ cup chopped fresh cilantro

Cilantro Yogurt
1 cup plain yogurt
2 tablespoons chopped fresh cilantro
1 teaspoon fresh lime juice

1 Heat oil in a large Dutch oven over medium-high heat. Add onions and cook until softened, 5 minutes. Add garlic, jalapeño, ginger, cumin, and curry; cook until fragrant, 30 seconds. Add lentils, water, salt, and pepper; bring to a boil. Reduce heat and simmer 30 minutes.

2 Stir in squash, potato, cauliflower, and carrots. Cook until vegetables are tender, 25 to 30 minutes more. Add peas and cook until heated through. Stir in cilantro. Serve with Cilantro Yogurt. Makes 6 servings.

Cilantro Yogurt: Combine yogurt, cilantro and lime juice in a small bowl.

PER SERVING		DAILY GOAL
Calories	268	2,000 (F), 2,500 (M)
Total Fat	5 g	60 g or less (F), 70 g or less (M)
Saturated fat	2 g	20 g or less (F), 23 g or less (M)
Cholesterol	5 mg	300 mg or less
Sodium	70 mg	2,400 mg or less
Carbohydrates	43 g	250 g or more
Protein	14 g	55 g to 90 g

NOTES

89

FESTIVE

STEWS

Plain or fancy and always perfect from the pot, each one of these succulent meat, seafood, and vegetable mélanges is ideal for do-ahead company fare. Your guests will swoon over our Roasted Seafood Stew with fresh lobster, Feijoada with black beans, pork, and spicy sausage, or our creamy Chicken and Porcini Mushroom Stew. Stewing has never been easier or more elegant!

GULF COAST SEAFOOD GUMBO WITH RICE

All you need is one slice of bacon to capture the smoky flavor typical of this zesty fish stew.

▼ *Low-fat*
▽ *Low-calorie*
  Prep time: 20 minutes
  Cooking time: 55 minutes
○ *Degree of difficulty: easy*

1 **slice bacon, chopped**
2 **tablespoons flour**
1 **large onion, chopped**
1 **red pepper, cored and cut into ½-inch dice**
1 **green pepper, cored and cut into ½-inch dice**
1 **teaspoon minced garlic**
¾ **teaspoon salt**
¼ **teaspoon freshly ground pepper**
¼ **teaspoon thyme**
⅛ **to ¼ teaspoon ground red pepper**

1 **can (13¾ or 14½ ounces) chicken broth, plus enough water to equal 3 cups or 3 cups Rich Chicken Stock (recipe, page 29)**
1 **cup sliced, frozen okra**
1 **cup drained and chopped canned tomatoes**
1 **cup chopped green onions**
1 **pound red snapper or catfish fillet, cut into 1½-inch chunks**
8 **ounces medium shrimp, peeled and deveined**
3 **cups cooked long-grain rice**

1 Cook bacon in a large, heavy Dutch oven over medium heat until crisp. Drain on paper towels. Reduce heat to medium-low. Stir flour into drippings and cook, stirring frequently, until mixture is a deep golden brown, about 12 to 15 minutes. (Be careful not to burn.)

2 Stir in onion, diced red and green peppers, garlic, salt, pepper, thyme, and ground red pepper. Cover and cook, stirring occasionally, until vegetables are tender, 10 minutes. Stir in broth, okra, tomatoes, and green onions. Return to a simmer and cook, covered, until mixture is thickened and vegetables are tender, 10 to

15 minutes. Stir in snapper and shrimp; cook until fish is opaque, 5 minutes more. Stir in bacon. Serve over cooked rice. Makes 6 servings.

PER SERVING WITH RICE		DAILY GOAL
Calories	300	2,000 (F), 2,500 (M)
Total Fat	6 g	60 g or less (F), 70 g or less (M)
Saturated fat	1 g	20 g or less (F), 23 g or less (M)
Cholesterol	78 mg	300 mg or less
Sodium	811 mg	2,400 mg or less
Carbohydrates	34 g	250 g or more
Protein	27 g	55 g to 90 g

NOTES

_____
_____
_____
_____
_____
_____
_____
_____
_____
_____

CLASSIC BOUILLABAISSE

▽ *Low-calorie*
Prep time: 30 minutes
Cooking time: 50 to 60 minutes
◐ *Degree of difficulty: moderate*

3 tablespoons extra-virgin olive oil
1 cup chopped onions
½ cup chopped leek
1 fennel bulb, chopped
1 tablespoon minced garlic
1 3-inch strip orange peel
¼ teaspoon thyme
   Pinch saffron threads
2 cans (14½ *or* 16 ounces each)
   tomatoes, drained
4 bottles (8 ounces each) clam juice
1 cup water
½ cup dry white wine
½ teaspoon salt
1 dozen cherrystone *or* littleneck
   clams, scrubbed and rinsed
12 ounces monkfish fillets, cubed
12 ounces red snapper fillets, cubed
12 ounces cod fillets, cubed
1 dozen medium shrimp, peeled and
   deveined

1 tablespoon pernod *or* ouzo
½ teaspoon freshly ground pepper
   Aioli (recipe at right)

1 Heat oil in a large Dutch oven over medium heat. Stir in onions, leek, and fennel; cook, stirring frequently, until vegetables are tender, about 10 minutes. Stir in garlic, orange peel, thyme, and saffron and cook 1 minute. Add tomatoes, clam juice, water, wine, and salt; bring to a boil. Reduce heat and simmer uncovered 30 minutes.

2 Increase heat to high and stir in clams. Cover and cook just until clams open, about 5 minutes. (Discard any unopened clams.) Stir in fish, shrimp, pernod, and pepper. Cover and simmer, just until fish is opaque, about 5 minutes more. Ladle into large bowls and top each serving with a dollop of Aioli. Makes 6 servings.

PER SERVING WITHOUT AIOLI		DAILY GOAL
Calories	323	2,000 (F), 2,500 (M)
Total Fat	10 g	60 g or less (F), 70 g or less (M)
Saturated fat	1 g	20 g or less (F), 23 g or less (M)
Cholesterol	113 mg	300 mg or less
Sodium	933 mg	2,400 mg or less
Carbohydrates	14 g	250 g or more
Protein	43 g	55 g to 90 g

AIOLI

Total prep time: 10 minutes
○ *Degree of difficulty: easy*

1 tablespoon minced garlic
½ teaspoon salt
2 large egg yolks, at room
   temperature
⅓ cup vegetable oil
⅓ cup olive oil
1 tablespoon fresh lemon juice
½ teaspoon freshly ground pepper

With the flat side of a knife, crush garlic with salt to form a paste. Whisk eggs yolks in a small bowl. In a thin, steady stream, pour in vegetable and olive oils, whisking constantly, until mixture is blended and thickened. Gradually whisk in lemon juice, pepper and garlic paste just to blend. Refrigerate until ready to serve. Makes ¾ cup.

PER TABLESPOON		DAILY GOAL
Calories	117	2,000 (F), 2,500 (M)
Total Fat	13 g	60 g or less (F), 70 g or less (M)
Saturated fat	2 g	20 g or less (F), 23 g or less (M)
Cholesterol	35 mg	300 mg or less
Sodium	93 mg	2,400 mg or less
Carbohydrates .	0 g	250 g or more
Protein .	1 g	55 g to 90 g

ROASTED SEAFOOD STEW

Prep time: 1½ hours
Cooking time: 70 minutes
Degree of difficulty: moderate

- **3 pounds ripe plum tomatoes, halved lengthwise and seeded**
- **1½ teaspoons salt, divided**
- **1 large head (2 ounces) whole garlic**
- **6 tablespoons extra-virgin olive oil, divided**
- **½ teaspoon freshly ground pepper**
- **2 cups chopped leeks**
- **1½ cups white wine**
- **1½ cups water**
- **1 bottle (8 ounces) clam juice**
- **1 onion, halved**
- **½ bay leaf**
- **1 teaspoon whole black peppercorns**
- **½ teaspoon thyme**
- **2 live lobsters (1¼ to 1½ pounds each)**
- **2 pounds monkfish fillets**
- **1 pound sea scallops**
- **2 pounds medium shrimp, peeled and deveined**
- **¼ cup brandy**

- **½ cup julienned fresh basil**
- **⅓ cup chopped fresh flat-leaf parsley**

1 Preheat oven to 325°F. Line a 15½x10½-inch jelly-roll pan with wax paper. Toss tomatoes in a large bowl with ½ teaspoon of the salt. Arrange tomatoes, cut side down in prepared pan. Remove outer skin from garlic; place in center of a piece of foil. Drizzle top with 1 tablespoon of the oil and wrap tightly. Bake tomatoes and garlic 1 hour. Cool. Separate garlic cloves and press each clove gently to remove soft pulp. Place in a small bowl and stir until smooth. Peel and coarsely chop tomatoes.

2 Heat 2 tablespoons of the oil in a small saucepan over medium heat. Add leeks; cover and cook until softened, 10 minutes. Stir in ½ teaspoon of the salt and the pepper. Remove from skillet.

3 Bring wine, water, and clam juice to a boil in a large Dutch oven. Add onion, bay leaf, peppercorns, and thyme; simmer 5 minutes. Add lobsters; cover and steam over medium heat 15 minutes. Remove lobsters; cool. Remove lobster meat, liver, and roe, if any; chop meat coarsely. Cover and refrigerate meat, liver, and roe. For broth, return shells to Dutch oven. Cover; simmer over low heat, stirring occasionally,

45 minutes. Strain broth from shells through a fine sieve. Increase oven temperature to 475°F. Combine broth and leek mixture in a large saucepan. Stir in tomatoes and garlic puree. Heat over medium heat until hot, 10 to 12 minutes. Cover and keep warm.

4 Heat remaining 3 tablespoons oil in a large roasting pan. Cut monkfish into 1½-inch cubes. Add to pan; stirring to coat with hot oil. Transfer to oven and roast 4 minutes, stirring once, until fish begins to turn opaque. Stir in scallops. Roast 4 to 6 minutes more, stirring halfway through, until opaque. Add shrimp and lobster meat; sprinkle with remaining ½ teaspoon salt and additional pepper, stir. Roast until shrimp turn pink, 2 to 3 minutes more. With a slotted spoon, transfer roasted fish to broth mixture; keep warm. Add brandy to seafood juices in roasting pan and cook over high heat until juices are reduced by half, 5 minutes. Stir into fish with basil and parsley. Makes 9 servings.

PER SERVING		DAILY GOAL	
Calories	399	2,000 (F), 2,500 (M)	
Total Fat	13 g	60 g or less (F), 70 g or less (M)	
Saturated fat	2 g	20 g or less (F), 23 g or less (M)	
Cholesterol	188 mg	300 mg or less	
Sodium	782 mg	2,400 mg or less	
Carbohydrates	17 g	250 g or more	
Protein	48 g	55 g to 90 g	

CIOPPINO

We love this famous version of fish and shellfish stew in a gutsy tomato sauce from the former John Clancy's seafood restaurant in New York City.

Prep time: 25 minutes
Cooking time: 55 to 60 minutes
○ *Degree of difficulty: easy*

⅓ cup olive oil
4 garlic cloves, minced
2 cups finely diced onions
1 cup white wine *or* vermouth
1 cup clam juice
1 can (35 ounces) tomatoes, drained, seeded, and chopped (reserve liquid)
½ cup chopped fresh basil
2 teaspoons salt
1½ teaspoons chopped fresh thyme *or* ½ teaspoon dried
½ teaspoon red pepper flakes
24 mussels, scrubbed, rinsed, and cleaned
8 ounces medium shrimp, shelled and deveined
1 pound cod fillet, cut into 2-inch cubes

1 tablespoon champagne, balsamic, *or* sherry vinegar
12 ounces linguine, cooked according to package directions

1 Heat oil in a large Dutch oven over medium-high heat. Add garlic and cook until fragrant, 30 seconds. Add onions and cook, stirring frequently, until softened, about 10 minutes. Add wine and cook until reduced by half. Add clam juice and tomatoes with liquid. Simmer uncovered 40 minutes. (Can be made ahead. Cool. Cover and refrigerate up to 2 days. Bring to a simmer over medium-low heat.)

2 Stir in basil, salt, thyme, and red pepper. Add mussels; cover and simmer until shells open, about 5 minutes. (Discard any unopened mussels.) Stir in shrimp and cod; cover and simmer until fish is opaque, about 5 minutes more. Stir in vinegar. Serve over linguine. Makes 6 servings.

PER SERVING		DAILY GOAL
Calories	501	2,000 (F), 2,500 (M)
Total Fat	15 g	60 g or less (F), 70 g or less (M)
Saturated fat	2 g	20 g or less (F), 23 g or less (M)
Cholesterol	89 mg	300 mg or less
Sodium	1,276 mg	2,400 mg or less
Carbohydrates	58 g	250 g or more
Protein	34 g	55 g to 90 g

NOTES

MONKFISH
POT AU FEU

Monkfish is similar to lobster in texture and flavor, but considerably less expensive. It is quite elegant in this lovely stew with baby vegetables.

Prep time: 40 minutes
Cooking time: 40 to 45 minutes
Degree of difficulty: moderate

1½ **cups water**
1 **cup dry vermouth**
1 **small onion, halved**
1 **carrot, cut into 2 or 3 pieces**
1 **sprig fresh thyme**
1 **small bay leaf**
6 **whole black peppercorns**
3 **tablespoons butter *or* margarine, softened and divided**
8 **ounces baby carrots, peeled**
8 **ounces small white onions, peeled**
2 **pounds monkfish fillets, about 1½ inches thick, trimmed**
¾ **teaspoon salt, divided**
½ **teaspoon white pepper, divided**
8 **ounces baby summer squash *or* medium summer squash, halved and cut into ¾-inch slices**
1 **tablespoon all-purpose flour**
⅔ **cup heavy *or* whipping cream**
2 **teaspoons Dijon mustard**
1 **head escarole, tough stems and large leaves removed, blanched**

1 Combine water, vermouth, onion, carrot, thyme, bay leaf, and peppercorns in a large stainless steel skillet; bring to a boil. Reduce heat and simmer 20 minutes. Strain liquid through a fine sieve into a bowl; set aside.

2 Melt 2 tablespoons butter in same skillet over medium heat. Add baby carrots and pearl onions; cook, stirring, 2 to 3 minutes. Add strained liquid; bring to a boil. Reduce heat and simmer covered 10 minutes.

3 Meanwhile, sprinkle monkfish with ¼ teaspoon of the salt and ¼ teaspoon of the white pepper. Add fish to skillet; cover and simmer gently about 3 minutes. With a wide spatula, turn fillets over. Add squash, cover, and simmer 10 to 12 minutes more or until fish is opaque and vegetables are tender. Transfer fish and vegetables with a slotted spoon to a warm serving platter; cover and keep warm.

4 Reduce liquid in skillet to ½ cup. Combine remaining 1 tablespoon butter and flour in a small bowl to form a smooth paste. Whisk into reduced liquid over medium heat. Whisk in cream, mustard, remaining ½ teaspoon salt and ¼ teaspoon white pepper. Simmer 1 minute. Drain excess liquid from fish and vegetables. Serve with sauce on a bed of blanched escarole. Makes 4 servings.

PER SERVING		DAILY GOAL
Calories	552	2,000 (F), 2,500 (M)
Total Fat	28 g	60 g or less (F), 70 g or less (M)
Saturated fat	15 g	20 g or less (F), 23 g or less (M)
Cholesterol	135 mg	300 mg or less
Sodium	693 mg	2,400 mg or less
Carbohydrates	25 g	250 g or more
Protein	38 g	55 g to 90 g

NOTES

_____

_____

_____

_____

_____

SEAFOOD TUREEN WITH SAUCE ROUILLE

You can use most any combination of fish fillets in this recipe.

▽ *Low-calorie*
Prep time: 30 minutes
Cooking time: 50 to 55 minutes
◒ *Degree of difficulty: moderate*

2 tablespoons olive oil
1 pound leeks, split lengthwise and sliced thin (about 5 cups)
1 fennel bulb (8 ounces), thinly sliced
½ cup finely chopped onion
3 bottles (8 ounces each) clam juice
1 cup white wine
1 cup water
1 can (14½ *or* 16 ounces) tomatoes, drained and chopped
¼ teaspoon salt
¼ teaspoon freshly ground pepper
¼ teaspoon thyme
½ bay leaf
1 3-inch strip orange peel

1 dozen cherrystone *or* littleneck clams, scrubbed and rinsed
8 ounces monkfish fillet, trimmed and cut up
8 ounces cod fillet, cut up
8 ounces red snapper fillet, cut up
8 ounces medium shrimp, peeled and deveined
1 loaf French bread, sliced and toasted
   Sauce Rouille (recipe at right)

1 Heat olive oil in a large Dutch oven over medium heat. Add leeks, fennel, and onion; cook stirring occasionally, until vegetables are tender, 15 minutes. Add clam juice, wine, water, tomatoes, salt, pepper, thyme, bay leaf, and orange peel; bring to a boil. Reduce heat and simmer uncovered 30 minutes.

2 Meanwhile, combine clams and ½ inch water in a medium saucepan. Cover and cook over high heat 3 to 6 minutes, just until clams open. (Discard any unopened clams.) Set aside.

3 Strain clam broth through a double layer of cheesecloth and add to stew; return to a brisk simmer. Add monkfish; cover and cook 1 minute. Add remaining fish,

shrimp, and clams; cook covered just until seafood is opaque, 3 to 5 minutes more. Remove bay leaf and orange peel. Serve in bowls with toasted French bread and Sauce Rouille. Makes 6 servings.

PER SERVING
WITHOUT BREAD
OR ROUILLE   DAILY GOAL

Calories	269	2,000 (F), 2,500 (M)
Total Fat	7 g	60 g or less (F), 70 g or less (M)
Saturated fat	1 g	20 g or less (F), 23 g or less (M)
Cholesterol	97 mg	300 mg or less
Sodium	631 mg	2,400 mg or less
Carbohydrates	18 g	250 g or more
Protein	33 g	55 g to 90 g

NOTES

_____

_____

_____

_____

_____

_____

_____

_____

SAUCE ROUILLE

This sauce is wonderful served with grilled fish and can be prepared ahead, covered, and refrigerated up to 2 days ahead.

Prep time: 30 minutes
Cooking time: 50 to 55 minutes
Degree of difficulty: easy

2 **large red peppers**
½ **cup boiling water**
¼ **to ½ teaspoon red pepper flakes**
2 **slices firm white bread, cubed**
½ **teaspoon salt**
½ **teaspoon freshly ground pepper**
¼ **cup extra-virgin olive oil**
1 **teaspoon minced garlic**

1 Prepare grill or preheat broiler. Grill or broil red peppers 3 inches from heat source for 20 minutes, turning every 5 minutes, until skin is evenly charred. Cover and cool 10 minutes, then remove and discard skin, membrane, and seeds.

2 Meanwhile, combine boiling water and red pepper flakes in a medium bowl. Add bread and soak until bread is softened and cooled, 10 minutes. Puree roasted peppers, soaked bread, salt, and pepper in a blender. With machine on, add oil in a thin, steady stream until mixture is smooth. Stir in garlic. Makes 1½ cups.

PER TABLESPOON		DAILY GOAL
Calories	28	2,000 (F), 2,500 (M)
Total Fat	2 g	60 g or less (F), 70 g or less (M)
Saturated fat	0 g	20 g or less (F), 23 g or less (M)
Cholesterol	0 mg	300 mg or less
Sodium	57 mg	2,400 mg or less
Carbohydrates	2 g	250 g or more
Protein	0 g	55 g to 90 g

NOTES

99

COUNTRY CAPTAIN

This chicken stew is designed for entertaining. If you prepare the chicken ahead, refrigerate the diced meat along with the homemade broth.

Prep time: 45 minutes plus chilling
Cooking time: 2 hours
Degree of difficulty: moderate

1 onion, chopped
3 ribs celery, chopped
24 black peppercorns
3 bay leaves
   Water
2 whole chickens (3 pounds each)
3 tablespoons unsalted butter
   (no substitutions)
2 tablespoons vegetable oil
2 cups chopped onions
1½ cups unpeeled, diced Granny
   Smith apples
1 cup diced green peppers
2 tablespoons minced garlic
1 tablespoon minced fresh ginger
3 tablespoons curry powder

1 teaspoon paprika
1 teaspoon freshly ground pepper
¼ teaspoon mace
¼ teaspoon cumin
⅛ teaspoon ground red pepper
3 cans (14½ *or* 16 ounces each)
   tomatoes, chopped and liquid
   reserved
2 teaspoons salt
¼ cup chopped fresh parsley
   Cooked rice
   Mango *or* peach chutney
8 slices bacon, cooked and crumbled
1 cup flaked coconut
1 cup chopped peanuts
1 cup currants

1 Combine onion, celery, peppercorns, bay leaves, and 8 cups water in a large stockpot; bring to a boil. Reduce heat and simmer 10 minutes. Add chickens to the stock pot with water just to cover. Return to a simmer; cook until chicken is cooked through, 45 minutes.

2 Remove chicken, reserving broth. Remove meat from chicken and chop into 1-inch pieces. Return skin and bones to broth and simmer 30 minutes more. Strain broth through a fine sieve or cheesecloth.

Discard solids. Refrigerate 4 hours or overnight. Skim off fat.

3 Melt butter with oil in a large Dutch oven over medium-high heat. Add onions, apples, peppers, garlic, and ginger. Cook, stirring, until onions are softened, 2 minutes. Reduce heat to medium, cover and cook 5 minutes more. Stir in curry powder, paprika, black pepper, mace, cumin, and ground red pepper; cook 1 minute. Stir in tomatoes with liquid, 2 cups reserved chicken broth, and salt; bring to a boil, Reduce heat and simmer 10 minutes. Add chopped chicken, cover and simmer 10 minutes more. Sprinkle with parsley and serve with rice and condiments (chutney, bacon, coconut, peanuts, and currants). Makes 8 servings.

PER SERVING WITHOUT CONDIMENTS		DAILY GOAL
Calories	383	2,000 (F), 2,500 (M)
Total Fat	18 g	60 g or less (F), 70 g or less (M)
Saturated fat	6 g	20 g or less (F), 23 g or less (M)
Cholesterol	120 mg	300 mg or less
Sodium	924 mg	2,400 mg or less
Carbohydrates	18 g	250 g or more
Protein	39 g	55 g to 90 g

OLD-TIME KENTUCKY BURGOO

An assortment of vegetables, savory meats, and poultry graces this zesty stew.

Prep time: 40 minutes
Cooking time: 2¼ hours
○ *Degree of difficulty: easy*

- 1 **whole chicken (3 pounds), cut up**
- 2 **slices thick-sliced bacon *or***
  4 regular slices, chopped
- 1 **pound lean, boneless beef chuck,**
  cut into 1-inch pieces
- 1¾ **teaspoons salt, divided**
  Freshly ground pepper
- ¼ **cup all-purpose flour**
- 1½ **cups chopped onions**
- 1 **cup chopped green peppers**
- ½ **cup chopped celery**
- 2 **teaspoons minced garlic**
- 1 **can (14½ *or* 16 ounces) tomatoes,**
  liquid reserved
- 2 **tablespoons Worcestershire sauce**
- ½ **teaspoon thyme**
- ¼ **teaspoon red pepper flakes**
- 1½ **pounds potatoes, peeled and cut**
  into 1-inch pieces
- 1 **pound carrots, peeled and cut into**
  1-inch pieces
- 1 **cup frozen baby lima beans,**
  thawed
- 1 **cup frozen whole-kernel corn,**
  thawed
- 1 **cup frozen cut okra, thawed**
- 2 **teaspoons red pepper sauce**
- ¼ **cup chopped fresh parsley**

1 Place chicken in a deep skillet with enough water to cover and ½ teaspoon of the salt; bring to a boil. Reduce heat and simmer 2 minutes. Remove from heat; cover and let stand 30 minutes.

2 Meanwhile, cook bacon in a large Dutch oven over medium-high heat until just crisp. Transfer with a slotted spoon to a medium bowl.

3 In a large bowl sprinkle beef with ½ teaspoon of the salt and ¼ teaspoon pepper. Add flour, tossing to coat meat, then shaking off excess. Add beef to drippings in Dutch oven and cook over medium-high heat until browned well on all sides, 7 minutes. Transfer beef to the bowl with bacon.

4 Add onions, green peppers, and celery to pan; cook until vegetables are softened, 5 minutes. Add garlic and cook until fragrant, 30 seconds. Add 4 cups chicken cooking liquid, the browned beef, bacon, tomatoes with liquid, Worcestershire, thyme, red pepper flakes, and remaining ¾ teaspoon salt; bring to a boil. Cover and simmer until beef is fork-tender, 1 hour and 20 minutes. Add potatoes, carrots, lima beans, and corn. Cook, covered, until vegetables are tender, 25 minutes.

5 Meanwhile, remove chicken from remaining cooking liquid. When cool enough to handle, remove skin and bones from chicken and discard. Cut meat into 1-inch pieces. Add chicken and okra to Dutch oven; cover and cook 10 minutes more until heated through. Stir in red pepper sauce. Sprinkle top with parsley. Makes 8 servings.

PER SERVING		DAILY GOAL
Calories	417	2,000 (F), 2,500 (M)
Total Fat	14 g	60 g or less (F), 70 g or less (M)
Saturated fat	5 g	20 g or less (F), 23 g or less (M)
Cholesterol	102 mg	300 mg or less
Sodium	862 mg	2,400 mg or less
Carbohydrates	38 g	250 g or more
Protein	35 g	55 g to 90 g

MADRAS
CHICKEN STEW

Because we caramelize a generous batch of sweet onions and toast our own blend of spices in a skillet, this version of chicken curry tastes fabulous.

▽ *Low-calorie*
Prep time: 1 hour
Cooking time: 1 hour
○ *Degree of difficulty: easy*

2 **pounds chicken breasts, quartered and skinned**
2 **pounds chicken legs, halved and skinned**
2½ **teaspoons salt, divided**
½ **teaspoon freshly ground pepper**
3 **tablespoons vegetable oil**
3½ **pounds onions, halved and sliced (8 to 10 cups)**
2 **tablespoons minced garlic**
2 **tablespoons all-purpose flour**
1 **can (14½ *or* 16 ounces) tomatoes, drained**
1 **cup canned chicken broth *or* Rich Chicken Stock (recipe, page 29)**
1 **bay leaf**
Fresh cilantro sprigs, for garnish

Spicy Curry Mix
1½ **teaspoons turmeric**
1 **teaspoon cumin**
1 **teaspoon freshly ground pepper**
½ **teaspoon cinnamon**
½ **teaspoon coriander**
½ **teaspoon ginger**
¼ **teaspoon cardamom**
¼ **teaspoon ground cloves**
¼ **teaspoon nutmeg**
¼ **teaspoon ground red pepper**
Cooked long-grain rice

1 Sprinkle chicken with 1 teaspoon of the salt and the pepper. Heat oil in a large deep skillet over high heat. Add a third of the pieces to the skillet and brown well on all sides. Transfer with a slotted spoon to a large, shallow baking pan. Repeat 2 more times with remaining chicken. Add onions to the skillet and cook over high heat, stirring occasionally, until onions are a deep caramel brown, 45 to 60 minutes.

2 Preheat oven to 350°F. Reduce heat in skillet to medium. Add garlic and Spicy Curry Mix and cook, stirring constantly, 3 minutes. Sprinkle in flour and cook, stirring constantly, 3 minutes more. Add tomatoes, chicken broth, remaining

1½ teaspoons salt, and bay leaf. Bring to a boil, stirring constantly, then pour mixture over chicken pieces. Cover and bake 45 minutes. Uncover and bake 15 minutes more. Remove bay leaf. Garnish with cilantro sprigs and serve with rice. Makes 9 servings.

Spicy Curry Mix: Combine all spices in a small heavy skillet. Toast over low heat, stirring constantly, until very fragrant and slightly darkened, about 4 minutes.

PER SERVING		DAILY GOAL
Calories	277	2,000 (F), 2,500 (M)
Total Fat	8 g	60 g or less (F), 70 g or less (M)
Saturated fat	1 g	20 g or less (F), 23 g or less (M)
Cholesterol	84 mg	300 mg or less
Sodium	920 mg	2,400 mg or less
Carbohydrates	20 g	250 g or more
Protein	30 g	55 g to 90 g

NOTES

_____

_____

_____

_____

_____

_____

_____

CHICKEN AND PORCINI MUSHROOM STEW

You only need an ounce of dried porcini mushrooms to give this creamy chicken stew its distinctive woodsy flavor. These mushrooms can be quite sandy, so be sure to soak them for 30 minutes. This recipe is lovely served with tender egg noodles.

Prep time: 25 minutes plus soaking
Cooking time: 35 to 40 minutes
Degree of difficulty: easy

- 1 ounce dried porcini mushrooms
- 1 cup lukewarm water
- 1 tablespoon vegetable oil
- 3 tablespoons butter *or* margarine, softened and divided
- 1 whole chicken (3½ pounds), cut into 8 pieces and skinned
- ½ cup all-purpose flour, divided
- ½ cup white wine
- 1 can (13¾ *or* 14½ ounces) chicken broth *or* 1¾ cups Rich Chicken Stock (recipe, page 29)
- 1 teaspoon salt
- ½ teaspoon freshly ground pepper
- ¼ teaspoon thyme
- 1 pound small white onions, peeled
- 1 pound carrots, peeled and sliced
- 8 ounces fresh mushrooms, quartered
- 1 package (10 ounces) frozen peas
- ½ cup heavy *or* whipping cream

1 Combine mushrooms and water in a small bowl. Soak 30 minutes. Remove mushrooms with a slotted spoon and set aside. Strain liquid through a double layer of cheesecloth; set the mushrooms aside and reserve the liquid.

2 Heat oil and 1 tablespoon butter in a large skillet over medium-high heat. Toss chicken pieces with ¼ cup of the flour in a large bowl and shake off excess. Add chicken to skillet and brown 5 minutes on each side. Add wine, chicken broth, reserved mushroom liquid, salt, pepper, thyme, onions, and carrots; bring to a boil. Reduce heat and simmer covered 25 minutes. Add porcini mushrooms, fresh mushrooms, and peas; cover and simmer until chicken and vegetables are tender, about 7 minutes more.

3 Transfer chicken and vegetables with a slotted spoon to a serving bowl; cover and keep warm. Add cream to skillet and bring to a simmer. Blend remaining 2 tablespoons butter with remaining ¼ cup flour in a small bowl to form a smooth paste. Gradually whisk into skillet and simmer 2 minutes. Pour sauce over chicken and vegetables, tossing to coat. Makes 6 servings.

PER SERVING		DAILY GOAL
Calories	456	2,000 (F), 2,500 (M)
Total Fat	21 g	60 g or less (F), 70 g or less (M)
Saturated fat	9 g	20 g or less (F), 23 g or less (M)
Cholesterol	132 mg	300 mg or less
Sodium	960 mg	2,400 mg or less
Carbohydrates	34 g	250 g or more
Protein	35 g	55 g to 90 g

NOTES

_____

_____

_____

_____

_____

_____

_____

BLACK BEAN CASSOULET

We've given this classic dish from France a south-of-the-border twist. The spicy pork and black bean stew is layered with sliced chicken and sweet sausage—perfect for autumn entertaining.

Prep time: 35 minutes plus soaking
Cooking time: 2 to 2½ hours
Degree of difficulty: easy

- 8 ounces dried black beans
   Water
- 3 tablespoons vegetable oil, divided
- 3 cups coarsely chopped onions
- 2 tablespoons chili powder
- 1 tablespoon minced jalapeño peppers
- 2 teaspoons minced garlic
   Salt
- 1 teaspoon cumin
- ½ teaspoon oregano
   Freshly ground pepper
- 1½ pounds lean pork shoulder, cubed
- ¼ cup stone-ground cornmeal
- 6 boneless chicken thighs (about 1¼ pounds)
- 1 pound sweet Italian sausage
- 1 cup plain dry bread crumbs
- ¼ cup chopped fresh cilantro

1 Rinse beans and pick over for small stones and shriveled beans. In a medium bowl, cover beans with 2 inches water and soak overnight. (To quick-soak: Combine beans with water to cover by 2 inches in a medium saucepan and bring to a boil; boil 2 minutes. Cover and let stand 1 hour.) Drain in a colander; set aside.

2 Heat 2 tablespoons of the oil in a large Dutch oven over medium heat. Add onions and cook until golden, about 15 minutes. Add chili powder, jalapeño, garlic, 1¼ teaspoons salt, cumin, oregano, and ¼ teaspoon pepper; cook, stirring, 2 minutes. Stir in beans and pork, then add 4 cups water; bring to a boil. Reduce heat and simmer covered 1½ to 2 hours or until beans and pork are tender. Stir in cornmeal and simmer until thickened, 5 minutes more.

3 Meanwhile, sprinkle chicken lightly with salt and pepper. Heat remaining 1 tablespoon oil in a large skillet over medium-high heat. Add chicken and cook until golden, 10 minutes per side. Set aside. Cook sausages in same skillet, turning occasionally, until evenly browned, 15 minutes. Cut chicken and sausages diagonally into ½-inch-thick slices.

4 Preheat oven to 350°F. Spread half of the pork and black bean mixture in a 13x9-inch baking dish. Top with half of the chicken and sausage slices. Repeat layering. Sprinkle top with bread crumbs. Bake 30 minutes or until heated through and bubbling. Let stand 5 minutes. Sprinkle with cilantro just before serving. Makes 10 servings.

PER SERVING		DAILY GOAL	
Calories	499	2,000 (F), 2,500 (M)	
Total Fat	25 g	60 g or less (F), 70 g or less (M)	
Saturated fat	7 g	20 g or less (F), 23 g or less (M)	
Cholesterol	107 mg	300 mg or less	
Sodium	775 mg	2,400 mg or less	
Carbohydrates	31 g	250 g or more	
Protein	37 g	55 g to 90 g	

RABBIT STEW WITH FENNEL

Domestic young rabbit is tender, subtly flavored and primarily white meat. It is available fresh or frozen and provides a distinctive alternative to chicken!

Prep time: 30 minutes
Cooking time: 70 minutes
○ *Degree of difficulty: easy*

1   **rabbit (about 2½ pounds), cut up**
1   **teaspoon salt, divided**
½   **teaspoon freshly ground pepper, divided**
2   **tablespoons vegetable oil**
2   **tablespoons olive oil, divided**
1   **cup chopped onions**
1   **cup chopped, peeled carrots**
2   **fennel bulbs (1 pound each), chopped, divided (reserve fronds)**
2   **teaspoons minced garlic**
1   **cup white wine**
1   **cans (13¾ or 14½ ounces each) chicken broth or 3½ cups Rich Chicken Stock (recipe, page 29)**
¼   **teaspoon thyme**
¼   **teaspoon rosemary**
¼   **teaspoon crushed fennel seeds**
1   **bay leaf**
⅓   **cup sliced shallots**
1   **teaspoon grated lemon peel**

1   Season rabbit with ½ teaspoon of the salt and ¼ teaspoon of the pepper. Heat 1 tablespoon of the oil in a large Dutch oven over high heat. Add rabbit and cook until browned well on both sides, 8 to 10 minutes. Transfer rabbit to a large bowl and set aside.

2   Reduce heat to medium-high and add onion, carrots, and half of the chopped fennel. Cook, stirring to scrape up any browned bits from pan, until vegetables are just tender, 6 minutes. Add garlic and cook 30 seconds. Add wine, chicken broth, thyme, rosemary, fennel seeds, bay leaf, remaining ½ teaspoon salt and ¼ teaspoon pepper, and rabbit pieces; bring to a boil. Reduce heat; cover and simmer until meat is slightly tender, 45 minutes.

3   Heat remaining 1 tablespoon oil in a skillet over medium-high heat. Add remaining chopped fennel; cook until tender, 5 to 7 minutes. Add shallots and cook until softened, 4 minutes. Add vegetables to stew and cook 10 minutes more.

4   Chop enough fennel fronds to make 2 tablespoons and combine with lemon peel in a small bowl. Sprinkle stew with lemon mixture just before serving. Makes 4 servings.

PER SERVING		DAILY GOAL	
Calories	506	2,000 (F), 2,500 (M)	
Total Fat	27 g	60 g or less (F), 70 g or less (M)	
Saturated fat	5 g	20 g or less (F), 23 g or less (M)	
Cholesterol	123 mg	300 mg or less	
Sodium	1,371 mg	2,400 mg or less	
Carbohydrates	16 g	250 g or more	
Protein	48 g	55 g to 90 g	

NOTES

107

DUCK AND RED WINE RAGOÛT

Young ducklings are available year round, fresh or frozen, and generally weigh between 3½ to 5 pounds. Fresh ducks can be refrigerated up to 2 to 3 days, with the giblets removed and stored separately. If you are purchasing your bird frozen, thaw it in the refrigerator.

Prep time: 40 minutes
Cooking time: 60 to 65 minutes
○ *Degree of difficulty: easy*

2   slices bacon, chopped
1   whole duck (4½ to 5 pounds), cut up and skin removed
1   teaspoon salt, divided
½   teaspoon freshly ground pepper, divided
2   cups chopped onions
2   teaspoons minced garlic
2   cups red wine
1   can (13¾ *or* 14½ ounces) chicken broth *or* 1¾ cups Rich Chicken Stock (recipe, page 29)
¾   teaspoon thyme
1   bay leaf

1   tablespoon vegetable oil
1   pound small fresh mushrooms, (halved if large)
1   pound carrots, peeled and cut into 2-inch pieces
8   ounces small white turnips, peeled and quartered
¼   cup chopped fresh parsley

1   Adjust oven rack to lowest position. Preheat oven to 375°F. Heat a large Dutch oven over medium-high heat. Add bacon and cook until just crisp. Transfer cooked bacon with a slotted spoon to a small bowl.

2   Sprinkle duck with ½ teaspoon of the salt and ¼ teaspoon of the pepper. Add 2 or 3 pieces of duck to the Dutch oven and brown well on all sides, about 8 minutes. Transfer with a slotted spoon to a large bowl. Repeat with remaining duck pieces.

3   Add the onions to the Dutch oven and cook until softened, 4 minutes. Add garlic and cook until fragrant, 30 seconds more. Add wine and broth; bring to a boil, scraping up browned bits from the bottom of pan. Add browned duck, thyme, bay leaf, and remaining ½ teaspoon salt and ¼ teaspoon pepper. Return to a boil, then cover and bake 45 minutes.

4   Meanwhile, heat oil in a large skillet over medium heat. Add mushrooms and cook until golden, 4 to 5 minutes. Add to stew along with carrots and turnips. Continue baking covered until duck and vegetables are tender, 15 to 20 minutes. Drain liquid from stew and transfer to same skillet. Cook until reduced and slightly thickened, then return to duck and vegetables. Spoon into bowls and sprinkle with parsley. Makes 4 servings.

PER SERVING		DAILY GOAL
Calories	481	2,000 (F), 2,500 (M)
Total Fat	23 g	60 g or less (F), 70 g or less (M)
Saturated fat	7 g	20 g or less (F), 23 g or less (M)
Cholesterol	149 mg	300 mg or less
Sodium	1,357 mg	2,400 mg or less
Carbohydrates	29 g	250 g or more
Protein	41 g	55 g to 90 g

NOTES

_____

_____

_____

_____

_____

_____

_____

VEAL BLANQUETTE

A classic French dish, this creamy stew always features small white onions and mushrooms. Slivered carrots and green peas add a touch of color and sweetness.

Prep time: 20 minutes
Cooking time: 1¼ hours
○ *Degree of difficulty: easy*

8 ounces small white onions, peeled
2 tablespoons butter *or* margarine
8 ounces fresh mushrooms, halved
   (quartered if large)
2 sprigs fresh parsley
1 sprig fresh thyme *or* ¼ teaspoon
   dried
1 whole clove
2 pounds veal stew meat, cut into
   1-inch cubes
1 can (13¾ *or* 14½ ounces) chicken
   broth *or* 1¾ cups Rich Chicken
   Stock (recipe, page 29)
¾ cup white wine
1¼ teaspoons salt
¼ teaspoon freshly ground pepper
3 medium carrots, peeled and cut
   diagonally into 1½-inch pieces
½ cup heavy *or* whipping cream
¼ cup all-purpose flour
¾ cup frozen peas, thawed
1 tablespoon chopped fresh dill *or*
   parsley
   Cooked long-grain rice

1 Heat onions with water to cover in a medium saucepan; bring to a boil over high heat and boil 3 minutes. Drain. Transfer to a medium bowl. Heat butter in a large Dutch oven over medium-high heat. Add mushrooms and cook, stirring, until liquid is evaporated and mushrooms begin to brown. Add to bowl with onions.

2 Prepare bouquet garni: Place parsley, thyme, and clove in a double thickness of cheesecloth. Tie up with a kitchen string and set aside.

3 Combine veal, chicken broth, wine, bouquet garni, salt, and pepper to any remaining drippings in Dutch oven; bring to a boil. Reduce heat to low and cover and simmer 45 minutes.

4 Stir in carrots, onions, and mushrooms; return to a boil. Reduce heat and simmer until veal and vegetables are tender, 30 minutes more. Discard bouquet garni.

5 Whisk cream and flour together in a cup until smooth. Stir into stew; bring to a boil, stirring constantly. Boil, stirring, 2 minutes. Just before serving, stir in peas and heat through. Stir in dill. Serve over rice. Makes 6 servings.

PER SERVING		DAILY GOAL
Calories	382	2,000 (F), 2,500 (M)
Total Fat	20 g	60 g or less (F), 70 g or less (M)
Saturated fat	10 g	20 g or less (F), 23 g or less (M)
Cholesterol	169 mg	300 mg or less
Sodium	1,022 mg	2,400 mg or less
Carbohydrates	16 g	250 g or more
Protein	33 g	55 g to 90 g

NOTES

_____

_____

_____

_____

_____

_____

_____

_____

VEAL STEW OSSO-BUCO STYLE

Traditionally this classic Italian stew is made with veal shanks, but we used boneless veal stew meat for convenience. To tingle the taste buds, serve the stew with a Gremolata, a fragrant combination of fresh parsley, lemon peel, and garlic.

For saffron risotto or rice, simply add a pinch of saffron to a basic recipe for either.

Prep time: 35 minutes
Cooking time: 2 to 2½ hours
Degree of difficulty: easy

3   tablespoons all-purpose flour
    Salt
    Freshly ground pepper
3   pounds veal stew meat, cubed
4   tablespoons olive oil, divided
1   cup chopped onions
½   cup chopped, peeled carrots
⅓   cup chopped celery
1   cup dry white wine
1   teaspoon minced garlic
1   3-inch strip lemon peel
1   can (14½ *or* 16 ounces) tomatoes, liquid reserved
1   tablespoon chopped fresh parsley
½   teaspoon thyme
½   teaspoon basil
¼   bay leaf
    Cooked saffron risotto or rice

Gremolata
1   tablespoon chopped fresh parsley
1   teaspoon grated lemon peel
½   teaspoon minced garlic

1   Combine flour, ½ teaspoon salt and ½ teaspoon pepper in a cup. Pat veal dry on paper towels, then coat with flour mixture and shake off excess. Heat half of the oil in a large skillet over medium-high heat. Add 7 or 8 pieces of veal to the skillet and brown well on all sides. Transfer with a slotted spoon to a large Dutch oven. Repeat with remaining veal, adding remaining oil as needed.

2   Reduce heat under skillet to medium. Add onions, carrots, and celery and cook until vegetables are softened, about 3 minutes. Add wine, garlic, and lemon peel. Cook 10 minutes, scraping up browned bits from bottom of the pan. Add to Dutch oven. Add tomatoes with liquid, parsley, thyme, basil, and bay leaf. Simmer, covered, 1½ hours, stirring occasionally and breaking up tomatoes with a spoon. Simmer uncovered 30 minutes more until veal is tender.

3   Season stew with salt and pepper to taste. Serve with saffron risotto or rice and Gremolata. Makes 6 servings.

Gremolata: Combine all ingredients in a small bowl.

PER SERVING		DAILY GOAL
Calories	422	2,000 (F), 2,500 (M)
Total Fat	21 g	60 g or less (F), 70 g or less (M)
Saturated fat	6 g	20 g or less (F), 23 g or less (M)
Cholesterol	197 mg	300 mg or less
Sodium	513 mg	2,400 mg or less
Carbohydrates	10 g	250 g or more
Protein	45 g	55 g to 90 g

NOTES

_____
_____
_____
_____
_____
_____
_____
_____

MEDITERRANEAN VEAL STEW

This rustic stew is brimming with the warm flavors of garlic, rosemary, olives, and fresh fennel. Serve with rice or noodles.

Prep time: 25 to 30 minutes
Cooking time: 2½ hours
Degree of difficulty: easy

4 tablespoons olive oil, divided
3 medium onions, sliced
3 garlic cloves, crushed
3 pounds veal stew meat, cubed
4 tablespoons all-purpose flour
2 cans (13¾ or 14½ ounces each)
   beef broth *or* 3½ cups Hearty
   Beef Stock (recipe, page 30)
¾ cup white wine
   Grated peel and juice of 1 lemon
1 bay leaf
¾ teaspoon rosemary, crushed
¼ teaspoon thyme
⅛ teaspoon freshly ground pepper
2 fennel bulbs, trimmed and cut into
   ½-inch-thick slices
1 pound fresh mushrooms, sliced
¼ cup chopped fresh parsley
½ cup pitted Niçoise *or* Gaeta olives

1 Heat 1 tablespoon of the oil in a large skillet over medium-high heat. Add onions and garlic; cook until tender, 5 minutes. With a slotted spoon, transfer onions to a 5-quart Dutch oven and set aside.

2 Add 2 more tablespoons of the oil to skillet. Add 7 or 8 pieces of veal to the skillet and brown well on all sides. Transfer with a slotted spoon to the Dutch oven. Repeat with remaining veal. Reduce heat to medium. Add remaining 1 tablespoon oil to the skillet. Add flour, stirring constantly to form a smooth paste. Add beef broth, wine, and lemon juice, stirring to scrape up any browned bits from the bottom of the pan. Stir in bay leaf, rosemary, thyme, and pepper; bring to a boil and boil 5 minutes.

3 Pour sauce over veal and onions in Dutch oven. Cover and cook over medium heat 1 hour. Add fennel and cook uncovered, stirring frequently, until meat is tender and stew is thickened, 1 hour more.

4 Add mushrooms to skillet; cover and cook over high heat 3 minutes, then cook uncovered until all liquid is evaporated.

5 Add mushrooms to stew with grated lemon peel and parsley. Remove bay leaf. (Can be made ahead. Cool. Cover and refrigerate up to 2 days. Reheat to simmering over medium heat.) Just before serving, stir in olives. Makes 6 servings.

PER SERVING		DAILY GOAL
Calories	445	2,000 (F), 2,500 (M)
Total Fat	17 g	60 g or less (F), 70 g or less (M)
Saturated fat	3 g	20 g or less (F), 23 g or less (M)
Cholesterol	191 mg	300 mg or less
Sodium	1,015 mg	2,400 mg or less
Carbohydrates	20 g	250 g or more
Protein	51 g	55 g to 90 g

NOTES

BOEUF BOURGUIGNON

The rich and mellow flavor of this classic beef stew, slowly braised in full-bodied, dry red wine with onions and mushrooms, definitely improves when prepared a day ahead.

Prep time: 1 hour
Cooking time: 2 to 2½ hours
Degree of difficulty: easy

- 3 **tablespoons all-purpose flour**
- ½ **teaspoon salt**
- ½ **teaspoon freshly ground pepper**
- 3 **pounds lean, boneless beef chuck, cut into 1½-inch cubes**
- 3 **tablespoons vegetable oil, divided**
- 2 **cups chopped onions**
- ½ **cup chopped, peeled carrot**
- 1 **teaspoon minced garlic**
- 2 **cups red wine**
- 1 **cup canned beef broth *or* Hearty Beef Stock (recipe, page 30)**
- 1 **tablespoon tomato paste**
- 1 **tablespoon chopped fresh parsley**
- ½ **teaspoon thyme**
- 2 **cups water**
- 16 **pearl onions, peeled**
- 4 **thick slices bacon, diced**
- 8 **ounces small fresh mushrooms**

1 Combine flour, salt, and pepper in a large bowl. Pat beef dry on paper towels and toss with flour mixture, shaking off excess flour. Heat half of the oil in a large skillet over medium-high heat. Add 7 or 8 pieces of beef to the skillet and brown well on all sides. Transfer with a slotted spoon to a large Dutch oven. Repeat with remaining beef, adding remaining oil as needed.

2 Reduce heat under skillet to medium. Add onions and carrot to skillet; cook until vegetables are softened, about 3 minutes. Add garlic and cook until fragrant, 30 seconds. Pour in wine and cook 2 minutes, scraping up browned bits from bottom of the pan. Add mixture to Dutch oven along with the broth, tomato paste, parsley, and thyme. Reduce heat to low and simmer, covered, until beef is almost tender, about 1½ hours.

3 Meanwhile, bring water to a boil in a large saucepan. Add onions and cook over medium heat until almost tender. Add bacon and cook 2 minutes more. Drain;

return onion mixture to pan and reduce heat to medium. Cook, stirring occasionally, until onions are lightly browned.

4 Add mushrooms, onions, and bacon to stew. Simmer uncovered until meat is tender, about 30 minutes more. If sauce is too thin, increase heat to high and boil until slightly thickened. (Can be made ahead. Cool. Cover and refrigerate up to 2 days. Skim fat. Reheat in 350°F oven 45 to 60 minutes.) Makes 8 servings.

PER SERVING		DAILY GOAL
Calories	377	2,000 (F), 2,500 (M)
Total Fat	21 g	60 g or less (F), 70 g or less (M)
Saturated fat	6 g	20 g or less (F), 23 g or less (M)
Cholesterol	115 mg	300 mg or less
Sodium	508 mg	2,400 mg or less
Carbohydrates	10 g	250 g or more
Protein	36 g	55 g to 90 g

NOTES

_____

_____

_____

_____

_____

_____

FEIJOADA

This dish from Brazil boasts a robust flavor from the slowly-simmered black beans, pork, and sausage. The sliced oranges, rice, and greens provide a good counterbalance to the rich taste of the stew.

Prep time: 45 minutes plus soaking
Cooking time: 2½ to 3 hours
○ *Degree of difficulty: easy*

- **1 pound dried black beans**
- **3 tablespoons vegetable oil, divided**
- **2 pounds boneless pork shoulder, cut into 1½-inch cubes**
- **2 smoked ham hocks (about 1½ pounds)**
- **4 cups water**
- **2 cups chopped onions**
- **1 tablespoon chopped garlic**
- **1 teaspoon dried pepper flakes**
- **1 can (14½ *or* 16 ounces) tomatoes, liquid reserved**
- **8 ounces garlic sausage *or* kielbasa, sliced ½-inch thick slices**
- **½ cup chopped fresh parsley**
- **1 teaspoon salt**

- **2 cups long-grain rice, cooked according to package directions**
- **2 packages (10 ounces each) frozen collard greens, cooked according to package directions**
- **5 oranges, peeled and sliced**

1 Rinse beans and pick over for small stones and shriveled beans. In a large bowl, cover beans with 2 inches water and soak overnight. (To quick-soak: Combine beans with water to cover by 2 inches in a large saucepan and bring to a boil; boil 2 minutes. Cover and let stand 1 hour.) Drain in a colander; set aside.

2 Pat pork dry on paper towels. Heat 2 tablespoons of the oil in a large skillet over high heat. Add 7 or 8 pieces of pork to the skillet and brown well on all sides. Transfer pork with a slotted spoon to a large Dutch oven. Repeat with remaining pork. Add soaked beans, ham hocks, and 4 cups water to Dutch oven; bring to a boil. Reduce heat, cover and simmer 2 hours. Remove ham hocks. When cool enough to handle, remove and discard skin and bones; shred meat and return to Dutch oven.

3 Heat remaining 1 tablespoon oil in same skillet over medium-high heat. Add onions and cook, stirring frequently, until softened, about 5 minutes. Stir in garlic and red pepper flakes; cook 30 seconds. Add tomatoes with liquid and cook 10 minutes more, breaking up tomatoes with a spoon. Add to stew with sausage, parsley, and salt. Simmer uncovered 30 minutes. Serve with rice, greens, and orange slices. Makes 8 servings.

PER SERVING		DAILY GOAL
Calories	896	2,000 (F), 2,500 (M)
Total Fat	36 g	60 g or less (F), 70 g or less (M)
Saturated fat	11 g	20 g or less (F), 23 g or less (M)
Cholesterol	113 mg	300 mg or less
Sodium	1,185 mg	2,400 mg or less
Carbohydrates	95 g	250 g or more
Protein	48 g	55 g to 90 g

NOTES

_____

_____

_____

_____

_____

_____

_____

BEEF AND OXTAIL STEW

The addition of meaty bones enhances the taste of this classic beef stew.

Prep time: 40 minutes
Cooking time: 3 hours
○ *Degree of difficulty: easy*

2 **tablespoons vegetable oil, divided**
3 **pounds lean, boneless beef chuck, cut into 2-inch cubes**
2 **pounds oxtails**
1½ **cups chopped onions**
¾ **cup chopped, peeled carrots**
¾ **cup chopped celery**
1 **tablespoon minced garlic**
2 **cups red wine**
1 **can (14½ *or* 16 ounces) tomatoes, liquid reserved**
1 **cup water**
2 **teaspoons salt**
1 **teaspoon thyme**
½ **teaspoon freshly ground pepper**
1¼ **pounds carrots, peeled and cut into 1-inch pieces**
5 **large celery ribs, cut into 1-inch pieces**
¼ **cup chopped fresh parsley**

1 Preheat oven to 325°F. Heat 1 tablespoon of the oil in a large skillet over medium-high heat. Pat beef chuck and oxtails dry with paper towels. Add 5 or 6 pieces of beef to the skillet and brown well on all sides. Transfer with a slotted spoon to a large Dutch oven. Repeat with remaining beef and oxtails, adding remaining 1 tablespoon oil as needed.

2 Add onions, chopped carrots, and celery to skillet; cook over medium heat, stirring occasionally, until vegetables are softened, 10 minutes. Add garlic and cook 1 minute more. Stir in wine, tomatoes with liquid, water, salt, thyme, and pepper, breaking up tomatoes with the back of a spoon; bring to a boil. Add to meat in Dutch oven and return to a boil. Cover and transfer to 325°F oven.

3 Cook 2 hours. Stir in carrot and celery pieces; cover and cook 30 minutes more. Stir and continue cooking uncovered until sauce is slightly thickened, about 30 minutes more. (Can be made ahead. Cool. Cover and refrigerate up to 2 days. Discard fat. Reheat in 350°F. oven 1 hour.) Sprinkle with parsley. Makes 8 servings.

PER SERVING		DAILY GOAL
Calories	409	2,000 (F), 2,500 (M)
Total Fat	20 g	60 g or less (F), 70 g or less (M)
Saturated fat	5 g	20 g or less (F), 23 g or less (M)
Cholesterol	111 mg	300 mg or less
Sodium	867 mg	2,400 mg or less
Carbohydrates	15 g	250 g or more
Protein	42 g	55 g to 90 g

NOTES

THE ART OF THE ELEGANT STEW

The secret to classic stewing is long, slow cooking to meld flavors and tenderize the meat. Here are the basics to keep in mind:

• **Preparing the meat:** To help brown the meat evenly, first, pat the meat dry with paper towels to remove excess moisture, then season, if desired. If the meat is to be coated with flour, sprinkle the meat with flour in a medium bowl, then transfer the meat to a strainer and shake out the excess flour. Too much flour will leave a pasty coating.

• **Browning the meat:** Whether you use a skillet or Dutch oven, be sure it has a large capacity. Heat your oil over medium-high or high heat; it's important that the oil is very hot— almost smoking.

Add no more than 7 or 8 pieces of meat at a time to the hot oil, making sure that the pieces do not touch. If you add too much meat at once, the oil temperature will drop and the meat will not brown properly. To brown the meat on all sides, turn with tongs.

• **Sautéing aromatic vegetables:** For many stew recipes, an assortment of vegetables is cooked in the pan drippings to flavor the stew. Cook the vegetables over medium or medium-high heat, until they are tender, about 5 minutes.

• **Simmering the stew:** Once you have combined the meat and vegetables, and added the liquid ingredients, it's esssential to bring the stew to a boil, whether you're stewing on the stove-top or in the oven.

Once a boil has been reached, transfer the stew to a preheated oven or reduce heat under the pot and bring it to a simmer. Simmer covered or uncovered as directed. This slow cooking is the key to a tender, flavorful stew. (When the heat is too high, the liquid will evaporate too quickly and the meat will not be properly tenderized.)

• **Finishing touches:** After the meat and vegetables are tender, if your sauce is too thin, transfer the meat and vegetables with a slotted spoon to a bowl and keep warm. Boil the remaining sauce over high heat until reduced and slightly thickened, about 5 to 10 minutes. Return meat and vegetables to pot, stirring to combine with sauce.

LAMB RAGOÛT

This wintery stew features high-fiber chick-peas, lima beans, and root vegetables.

Prep time: 30 minutes plus soaking
Cooking time: 2 to 2½ hours
Degree of difficulty: easy

1½ cups dried chick-peas (garbanzo beans)
Water
5 teaspoons vegetable oil, divided
1 cup chopped onions
2½ pounds boneless lamb shoulder, cut into 1½-inch cubes
2 teaspoons minced garlic
1½ teaspoons salt
¾ teaspoon freshly ground pepper
½ teaspoon thyme
½ bay leaf
2 cans (13¾ *or* 14½ ounces each) chicken broth *or* 3½ cups Rich Chicken Stock (recipe, page 29)
1 can (35 ounces) tomatoes, chopped and liquid reserved
1 pound turnips, peeled and julienned
12 ounces carrots, peeled and julienned
1 package (10 ounces) frozen baby lima beans
¼ cup chopped fresh parsley

1 Rinse chick-peas and pick over for small stones and shriveled beans. In a large bowl, cover chick-peas with 2 inches water and soak overnight. (To quick-soak: Combine chick-peas with water to cover by 2 inches in a large saucepan and bring to a boil; boil 2 minutes. Cover and let stand 1 hour.) Drain in a colander; set aside.

2 Heat 2 teaspoons of the oil in a large skillet over high heat. Add onions and cook until tender, about 5 minutes. Transfer with a slotted spoon to a large Dutch oven.

3 Pat lamb dry with paper towels. Heat remaining 3 teaspoons oil in same skillet over high heat. Add 7 or 8 pieces of lamb to the skillet and brown well on all sides. Transfer lamb with a slotted spoon to Dutch oven. Repeat with remaining lamb.

4 Add 2 cups water to skillet and simmer over high heat 1 minute, scraping up browned bits from bottom of the pan. Add pan juices to Dutch oven. Stir in soaked chick-peas, garlic, salt, pepper, thyme, bay leaf, and chicken broth; bring to a boil.

Reduce heat, cover, and simmer 1 hour, skimming occasionally. Add tomatoes with liquid and simmer covered 30 minutes. Add turnips, carrots, and lima beans; cover and cook 30 minutes more or until lamb and chick-peas are tender. Sprinkle with parsley. Makes 10 servings.

PER SERVING		DAILY GOAL
Calories	524	2,000 (F), 2,500 (M)
Total Fat	29 g	60 g or less (F), 70 g or less (M)
Saturated fat	11 g	20 g or less (F), 23 g or less (M)
Cholesterol	82 mg	300 mg or less
Sodium	824 mg	2,400 mg or less
Carbohydrates	37 g	250 g or more
Protein	29 g	55 g to 90 g

NOTES

119

WILD ABOUT

CHILI

Catch chili fever! In this collection of fiery treats, we've cooked up only the best bowls of red! We've got fast Champion Chili Con Carne, Chunky Chicken Chili with beans and succotash, and Cincinnati Chili with all the fixin's. You'll also love our meatless versions, like Big Barley Chili packed with grains, and Totally Vegetarian Chili with smoky chipotle chilies. We know you love your chili hot, so pull up a chair and dig right in!

MARKET STREET CHILI

This bowl of fire from Dudley Moore's Los Angeles restaurant is justly famous. This chili recipe is definitely designed to feed a crowd, but it can also be cut in half easily.

Prep time: 1 hour
Cooking time: 1½ to 2 hours
O *Degree of difficulty: easy*

8 ounces thick-sliced bacon, diced
2 large onions, chopped fine
2 tablespoons minced garlic
2 tablespoons vegetable oil
4 pounds lean, boneless beef chuck, diced into ½-inch pieces
2 pounds boneless pork butt *or* shoulder, diced into ½-inch pieces
2 cans (29 *or* 32 ounces each) pureed tomatoes
2 bottles (12 ounces each) ale *or* beer
1 cup water
½ cup plus 2 tablespoons chili powder
½ cup cumin
2 tablespoons oregano
1 tablespoon ground red pepper
1 tablespoon salt
3 jalapeño peppers, seeded and minced
¼ cup fresh lime juice
Shredded cheddar cheese, chopped onion, and sour cream, for garnish

1 Cook bacon in a large skillet until just crisp. Add onions and garlic and cook until softened, about 5 minutes. Transfer with a slotted spoon to a large Dutch oven.

2 Heat oil in same skillet over medium-high heat. Add 7 or 8 pieces of meat to the skillet and brown over all sides. Transfer with a slotted spoon to the Dutch oven. Repeat with remaining meat in batches.

3 Add tomatoes, ale, water, chili powder, cumin, oregano, red pepper, salt, and jalapeños, stirring well to combine; bring to a boil. Reduce heat and simmer uncovered until meat is very tender, 1½ to 2 hours. (Can be made ahead. Cover and refrigerate up to 3 days or freeze up to 1 month.) Stir in lime juice. Spoon into bowls and serve with garnishes. Makes 14 servings.

PER SERVING		DAILY GOAL
Calories	551	2,000 (F), 2,500 (M)
Total Fat	33 g	60 g or less (F), 70 g or less (M)
Saturated fat	11 g	20 g or less (F), 23 g or less (M)
Cholesterol	41 mg	300 mg or less
Sodium	1,279 mg	2,400 mg or less
Carbohydrates	23 g	250 g or more
Protein	42 g	55 g to 90 g

NOTES

CINCINNATI CHILI

A classic from the Midwest, this fragrant chili with a touch of cinnamon and chocolate is slowly simmered to a sauce-like consistency and served on top of spaghetti. Local tradition calls for a variety of toppings such as shredded cheddar cheese, chopped onions, and oyster crackers.

▼ *Low-fat*
Prep time: 25 minutes
Cooking time: 3 hours
O *Degree of difficulty: easy*

2   **pounds lean (95%) ground beef**
1   **quart water**
2   **medium onions, finely grated**
2   **cans (8 ounces each) tomato sauce**
5   **whole allspice**
5   **whole cloves**
4   **garlic cloves, minced**
¼   **cup chili powder**
2   **tablespoons white *or* cider vinegar**
1   **bay leaf**
½   **square (½ ounce) unsweetened chocolate, chopped**
2   **teaspoons Worcestershire sauce**
1½   **teaspoons salt**
1   **teaspoon cinnamon**
1   **teaspoon cumin**
½   **teaspoon ground red pepper**
1   **pound spaghetti, cooked according to package directions**

1 Combine beef and water in a 4-quart saucepan and stir until meat is separated; bring to a boil. Reduce heat and simmer 30 minutes. Add onions, tomato sauce, allspice, cloves, garlic, chili powder, vinegar, bay leaf, chocolate, Worcestershire, salt, cinnamon, cumin, and pepper. Bring to a boil, stirring, then reduce heat and simmer uncovered 2 hours.

2 When the chili has thickened slightly, cover and simmer 1 hour more. Serve over spaghetti. Makes 6 servings.

PER SERVING		DAILY GOAL
Calories	535	2,000 (F), 2,500 (M)
Total Fat	9 g	60 g or less (F), 70 g or less (M)
Saturated fat	2 g	20 g or less (F), 23 g or less (M)
Cholesterol	73 mg	300 mg or less
Sodium	1,404 mg	2,400 mg or less
Carbohydrates	75 g	250 g or more
Protein	40 g	55 g to 90 g

NOTES

BOWL O' RED

Here's the Lone Star State favorite. Always prepared with cubed beef, without tomatoes or beans, this fiery brew gets its color from the chili powder. *Also pictured on page 120.*

Prep time: 30 minutes
Cooking time: 2 hours
Degree of difficulty: easy

3 pounds boneless, lean beef chuck, cut into ½-inch cubes
1 teaspoon salt, divided
¾ teaspoon freshly ground pepper, divided
3 tablespoons vegetable oil, divided
4 cups chopped onions
1 tablespoon minced garlic
3 tablespoons chili powder
3 tablespoons yellow cornmeal
1 tablespoon cumin
2 teaspoons oregano
¼ teaspoon ground red pepper
1 can (13¾ *or* 14½ ounces) beef broth plus enough water to equal 3 cups *or* 3 cups Hearty Beef Stock (recipe, page 30)
1 tablespoon brown sugar

1 Season beef cubes with ½ teaspoon of the salt and ¼ teaspoon of the freshly ground pepper. Heat 1 tablespoon of the oil in a large Dutch oven over high heat. Divide beef into three batches. Add a batch of beef and brown well on all sides, adding oil as needed, 6 minutes per batch. Repeat with remaining 2 batches. Transfer beef with a slotted spoon to a large bowl and set aside.

2 Add onions to Dutch oven and cook over medium-high heat, scraping up any browned bits from the bottom of the pan, until onions are tender, 5 minutes. Stir in garlic, chili powder, cornmeal, cumin, oregano, and red pepper; cook 30 seconds. Add beef broth and water, reserved meat, and remaining ½ teaspoon salt and remaining ¼ teaspoon freshly ground pepper.

3 Bring chili to a boil, then cover and simmer, stirring occasionally, over low heat until meat is tender, 1½ to 2 hours. Makes 4 servings. Garnish with chopped red or green pepper, if desired.

PER SERVING		DAILY GOAL
Calories	489	2,000 (F), 2,500 (M)
Total Fat	25 g	60 g or less (F), 70 g or less (M)
Saturated fat	7 g	20 g or less (F), 23 g or less (M)
Cholesterol	148 mg	300 mg or less
Sodium	895 mg	2,400 mg or less
Carbohydrates	19 g	250 g or more
Protein	47 g	55 g to 90 g

HOW TO HANDLE FRESH AND DRIED CHILIES

• When chopping or removing the seeds from hot chilies, the best way to protect yourself from the heat of the pepper is to wear rubber gloves.

• After working with chilies, thoroughly wash your hands and gloves with hot soapy water.

• If your hands come in direct contact with chilies, take care never to rub your hands against your eyes or mouth.

• Keep in mind, the heat in the chili comes from the seeds; handle them with care.

WHEATBERRY CHILI

Wheatberries are whole, unprocessed kernels of wheat. Once cooked, they have a wonderful meaty texture. We think you'll love this.

Prep time: 25 minutes plus chilling
Cooking time: 3½ hours
○ *Degree of difficulty: easy*

3 **tablespoons vegetable oil, divided**
1 **pound boneless, lean beef chuck, cubed**
1 **pound lean pork shoulder, cubed**
2 **cups chopped onions**
2 **tablespoons chili powder**
1 **tablespoon minced garlic**
2 **teaspoons cumin**
1 **teaspoon red pepper flakes**
2 **teaspoons salt, divided**
1 **can (14½ *or* 16 ounces) tomatoes, liquid reserved**
1 **can (13¾ *or* 14½ ounces) beef broth *or* 1¾ cups Hearty Beef Stock (recipe, page 30)**
1 **cup wheatberries**

4 **cups water**
2 **slices bacon**
Sliced green onions, for garnish

1 Heat 1 tablespoon of the oil in a large Dutch oven over high heat. Pat meat dry with paper towels. Add 7 or 8 pieces of meat to the Dutch oven and brown well on all sides. Transfer meat with a slotted spoon to a large bowl. Repeat with remaining meat, adding remaining oil as needed.

2 Add onions to Dutch oven and cook, stirring occasionally, until translucent, about 5 minutes. Add chili powder, garlic, cumin, red pepper flakes, and 1 teaspoon of the salt. Cook 1 minute more. Return meat to Dutch oven. Add the tomatoes with liquid and beef broth; bring to a boil. Reduce heat, cover, and simmer 1½ hours. Refrigerate overnight. Skim off fat.

3 Combine wheatberries, water, bacon, and remaining 1 teaspoon salt in a medium saucepan; bring to a boil. Reduce heat and simmer covered 1½ hours. Drain in a colander; discard bacon. Add wheatberries to chili; bring to a boil. Reduce heat and simmer uncovered 30 minutes more or until heated through. Serve with chopped green onions. Makes 8 servings.

PER SERVING WITHOUT GARNISHES		DAILY GOAL
Calories	354	2,000 (F), 2,500 (M)
Total Fat	18 g	60 g or less (F), 70 g or less (M)
Saturated fat	5 g	20 g or less (F), 23 g or less (M)
Cholesterol	77 mg	300 mg or less
Sodium 1,032	927 mg	2,400 mg or less
Carbohydrates	22 g	250 g or more
Protein	27 g	55 g to 90 g

NOTES

VENISON COWBOY CHILI

This is for serious chili lovers, a stick-to-your-ribs, ranch-hand's favorite. The rich flavor of the ground game meat may keep your crew guessing but will win raves.

Ⓜ *Microwave*
▼ *Low-fat*
  Prep time: 20 minutes
  Cooking time: 1½ hours
◯ *Degree of difficulty: easy*

3 **tablespoons vegetable oil, divided**
2 **pounds ground venison *or* lean (95%) ground beef**
2 **cups chopped onions**
1 **cup chopped green peppers**
2 **tablespoons yellow cornmeal**
1 **tablespoon minced garlic**
2 **tablespoons chili powder**
1 **teaspoon cumin**
1 **teaspoon oregano**
¼ **teaspoon ground red pepper (optional)**
1 **can (14½ *or* 16 ounces) tomatoes, liquid reserved**
1 **can (4 ounces) whole green chilies, drained and chopped**
1 **bottle (12 ounces) beer**
2 **teaspoons salt**
¼ **teaspoon freshly ground pepper**
2 **cans (16 ounces each) pinto beans, drained and rinsed**

1 Heat 1 tablespoon of the oil in a large Dutch oven over high heat. Add half the venison and cook, breaking up meat with a spoon, until browned, 6 to 8 minutes. Transfer to a medium bowl with a slotted spoon. Brown the remaining venison with another tablespoon of the oil and add to the bowl.

2 Add remaining 1 tablespoon oil to Dutch oven. Add onions and green peppers; cook until vegetables are tender, 5 minutes. Add cornmeal, garlic, chili powder, cumin, oregano, and red pepper; cook until fragrant, 30 seconds. Add tomatoes with liquid, breaking up with a spoon. Then add chilies, beer, salt, pepper, and browned meat; bring to a boil. Cover and simmer until thickened, 1½ hours. (Can be made ahead. Cool. Cover and refrigerate overnight. To reheat, transfer chili to a large microwave-proof bowl. Cover and microwave on high (100%

power) 6 minutes, stirring once, until heated through.) Makes 6 servings.

PER SERVING		DAILY GOAL
Calories	401	2,000 (F), 2,500 (M)
Total Fat	12 g	60 g or less (F), 70 g or less (M)
Saturated fat	2 g	20 g or less (F), 23 g or less (M)
Cholesterol	129 mg	300 mg or less
Sodium	1,313 mg	2,400 mg or less
Carbohydrates	30 g	250 g or more
Protein	43 g	55 g to 90 g

CHAMPION CHILI CON CARNE

Here's the one-pot classic with ground beef. Ready in minutes, this chili makes a perfect filling for enchiladas, burritos, or tostadas.

Ⓜ *Microwave*
  Prep time: 7 minutes
  Cooking time: 30 minutes
◯ *Degree of difficulty: easy*

1 **tablespoon vegetable oil**
2 **cups finely chopped onions**
2 **tablespoons minced garlic**
¼ **cup chili powder**
2 **tablespoons cumin**
2 **teaspoons salt**

½ teaspoon freshly ground pepper
¼ to ½ teaspoon ground red pepper
3 pounds lean ground beef
1 can (28 ounces) tomatoes, coarsely chopped and liquid reserved
¼ cup chopped fresh cilantro

1 Heat oil in a large skillet over medium heat. Add onions and cook until softened, 3 minutes. Add garlic and cook until fragrant, 30 seconds. Stir in chili powder, cumin, salt, pepper, and ground red pepper and cook 1 minute.

2 Add beef and cook, stirring to break up meat with a spoon, until no longer pink, 5 minutes. Stir in tomatoes with liquid and simmer until thickened, 20 minutes. (Can be made ahead. Cool. Cover and refrigerate up to 24 hours. To reheat, transfer to a large microwave-proof bowl. Cover and microwave on high—100% power—12 minutes, stirring every 3 minutes, or until hot.) Stir in cilantro. Makes 8 servings.

PER SERVING		DAILY GOAL
Calories	521	2,000 (F), 2,500 (M)
Total Fat	38 g	60 g or less (F), 70 g or less (M)
Saturated fat	14 g	20 g or less (F), 23 g or less (M)
Cholesterol	128 mg	300 mg or less
Sodium	872 mg	2,400 mg or less
Carbohydrates	11 g	250 g or more
Protein	32 g	55 g to 90 g

HOT STUFF

Here's the scoop on our favorite chilies:

FRESH CHILIES are available in Latin American markets and the produce section of many supermarkets.

• **Jalapeño:** Medium-hot. This is the most common fresh chili. Widely available and versatile, these chilies are usually sold green, but the equally hot red ones are more mature.

• **Serrano:** Very hot. If you want an extra blast of heat, substitute this chili for the jalapeño. Its appearance is similar to that of the jalapeño, but it has a thinner skin.

DRIED CHILIES are more widely available in supermarkets, specialty food stores, and Latin American markets. Dried (and canned) chilies can also be ordered from Mo-Hotta Mo-Betta, 800-462-3220.

• **Pasilla (Chili Negro):** Mild to medium-hot. Reddish-black skin, with a deep, tangy flavor.

• **Chipotle:** Very hot. Also available canned in adobo, these chilies are dried, smoked jalapeños with a rich, smoky flavor.

• **Ancho:** Mild to medium-hot. These dried poblano chilies have a deep, rich flavor with an undertone of sweetness.

• **Chile de Àrbol:** Very hot. An orange-red dried chili with a straight-forward and uncomplicated flavor.

• **New Mexican (California) Chili:** Mild to medium-hot. Red-skinned, with a slightly tart flavor.

TEXAS BLACK BEAN CHILI

Make a double batch of this satisfying chili and freeze half for another meal.

Prep time: 30 minutes plus standing
Cooking time: 1¼ hours
○ *Degree of difficulty: easy*

1 **pound dried black beans**
   Water
2 **smoked ham hocks**
      (about 1½ pounds)
3 **teaspoons salt, divided**
2 **tablespoons vegetable oil**
1 **pound lean (90%) ground beef**
2 **cups chopped onions**
1 **cup chopped, peeled carrots**
1 **cup diced red *or* green pepper**
2 **tablespoons chili powder**
1 **tablespoon minced garlic**
2 **teaspoons cumin**
½ **teaspoon ground red pepper**
   Diced fresh tomato and sour
      cream, for garnish

1 Rinse beans and pick over for small stones and shriveled beans. In a large bowl, cover beans with 2 inches water and soak overnight. (To quick-soak: Combine beans with water to cover by 2 inches in a large saucepan and bring to a boil; boil 2 minutes. Cover and let stand 1 hour.) Drain in a colander.

2 Transfer beans to a large Dutch oven with 7 cups water and ham hocks; bring to a boil. Reduce heat, cover, and simmer 30 minutes. Add 2 teaspoons of the salt; cook covered until beans are tender, 30 minutes more.

3 Heat oil in a large skillet over medium-high heat. Add beef and brown, stirring to break up meat. Add onions, carrots, diced pepper, and remaining 1 teaspoon salt. Cook, stirring, 10 minutes. Stir in chili powder, garlic, cumin, and ground pepper and cook 1 minute more. Remove ham hocks from Dutch oven. If beans are very soupy, remove 1 cup liquid. Add beef mixture to beans and simmer 10 minutes. Serve with diced tomatoes and sour cream. Makes 6 servings.

PER SERVING		DAILY GOAL
Calories	540	2,000 (F), 2,500 (M)
Total Fat	18 g	60 g or less (F), 70 g or less (M)
Saturated fat	5 g	20 g or less (F), 23 g or less (M)
Cholesterol	168 mg	300 mg or less
Sodium	1,325 mg	2,400 mg or less
Carbohydrates	58 g	250 g or more
Protein	40 g	55 g to 90 g

NOTES

DOUBLE-HEADER CHILI

Here's a no-fuss barrel of chili that makes 2 meals at once, with or without beans. Freeze a batch, but be sure to allow the chili to thaw overnight in the refrigerator before reheating.

▽ *Low-calorie*
  Prep time: 10 minutes
  Cooking time: 2 to 2½ hours
○ *Degree of difficulty: easy*

4	pounds lean, boneless beef chuck, cut into 1-inch cubes
6	cups chopped onions
1	bottle (12 ounces) beer
½	cup chili powder
6	tablespoons tomato paste
2	tablespoons seeded, minced jalapeño peppers
2	tablespoons minced garlic
2½	teaspoons salt
1	teaspoon freshly ground pepper

Preheat oven to 325°F. Combine beef, onions, beer, chili powder, tomato paste, jalapeño, garlic, salt, and pepper in a large, heavy Dutch oven. Cover tightly and roast until meat is very tender, 2 to 2½ hours. (Can be made ahead. Cover and refrigerate up to 3 days or freeze up to 1 month.) Makes 10 servings.

PER CUP SERVING		DAILY GOAL
Calories	344	2,000 (F), 2,500 (M)
Total Fat	15 g	60 g or less (F), 70 g or less (M)
Saturated fat	5 g	20 g or less (F), 23 g or less (M)
Cholesterol	118 mg	300 mg or less
Sodium	833 mg	2,400 mg or less
Carbohydrates	16 g	250 g or more
Protein	37 g	55 g to 90 g

Chili with Beans: Combine 5½ cups Double-Header Chili with 1 can (19 ounces) red kidney beans, drained and rinsed, in a large saucepan. Cook over medium heat until heated through, 10 minutes. Makes 6 servings.

PER SERVING		DAILY GOAL
Calories	300	2,000 (F), 2,500 (M)
Total Fat	11 g	60 g or less (F), 70 g or less (M)
Saturated fat	4 g	20 g or less (F), 23 g or less (M)
Cholesterol	84 mg	300 mg or less
Sodium	690 mg	2,400 mg or less
Carbohydrates	20 g	250 g or more
Protein	31 g	55 g to 90 g

RED HOT CHILI POWDER

There's a wide variety of commercial chili powders on the market. Most are a blend of dried, ground chili peppers, garlic salt, cumin, and oregano. If the flavor of chili pepper is what you have in mind, pure powdered chilies such as ancho are also available ranging from mild to hot, and can be substituted in any of our recipes.

NOTES

MEXICAN MOLE CHILI

One of the most famous sauces in Mexican cuisine is mole (mo-lay), a fragrant blend of onions, garlic, assorted chilies, ground nuts and seeds, and chocolate.

Ⓜ *Microwave*
Prep time: 45 minutes plus standing and chilling
Cooking time: 1¼ hours
○ *Degree of difficulty: easy*

- 3 **dried ancho chilies, seeded and stems removed**
- 3 **dried New Mexican chilies, seeded and stems removed**
- 1 **dried de arbol chile, seeded and stems removed (optional)**
  Boiling water
- ¼ **cup hulled, unsalted pumpkin seeds**
- ¼ **cup chopped almonds**
- 2 **tablespoons vegetable oil, divided**
- 3 **pounds boneless, skinless turkey breast, cut into 1-inch cubes**
- 1½ **teaspoons salt, divided**
- ¼ **teaspoon freshly ground pepper**
- 2 **cups chopped onions**
- 1 **tablespoon minced garlic**
- ½ **teaspoon cinnamon**
- ½ **teaspoon coriander**
  Pinch cloves
- ½ **cup tomato sauce**
- 1 **square (1 ounce) semisweet chocolate, chopped**
- 1 **dry corn tortilla *or* 1 slice dry white bread, broken up**
- ¼ **cup raisins**
- 3 **cups canned chicken broth *or* Rich Chicken Stock (recipe, page 29), divided**

1 Combine the chilies in a large skillet; toast over medium-high heat, turning frequently, until fragrant and pliable, 2 minutes. (Be careful not to get peppery smoke in your eyes.) Transfer chilies to a medium bowl and add enough boiling water to cover. Let stand until softened, 30 minutes. Drain.

2 Meanwhile, combine pumpkin seeds and almonds in same skillet. Heat, stirring, over medium heat until toasted and seeds are popped, 6 to 7 minutes. Set aside.

3 Heat 1 tablespoon of the oil in a large Dutch oven over high heat. Sprinkle turkey with 1 teaspoon salt and pepper. Add 7 or 8 pieces of turkey to the pot and brown well on all sides, about 5 minutes. Transfer with a slotted spoon to a large bowl. Repeat with remaining turkey in batches, adding remaining oil as needed.

4 Reduce heat to medium and add onions to Dutch oven; cook until tender, 5 minutes. Add garlic, cinnamon, coriander, and cloves; cook until fragrant, 30 seconds. Stir in tomato sauce, then remove from heat and transfer to a blender. Add softened chilies, toasted nuts, chocolate, tortilla, raisins, and ½ cup chicken broth. Puree until very smooth, adding additional broth if necessary.

5 Return sauce mixture to Dutch oven. Stir in browned turkey, remaining chicken broth, and remaining ½ teaspoon salt; bring to a boil. Cover and simmer stirring occasionally, until turkey is very tender, 1¼ hours. Cool. Cover and refrigerate overnight. (To reheat, transfer chili to a large microwave-proof bowl. Cover and microwave on high—100% power— 10 minutes, stirring twice, until heated through.) Makes 8 servings.

PER SERVING		DAILY GOAL	
Calories	358	2,000 (F), 2,500 (M)	
Total Fat	11 g	60 g or less (F), 70 g or less (M)	
Saturated fat	2 g	20 g or less (F), 23 g or less (M)	
Cholesterol	106 mg	300 mg or less	
Sodium	1,033 mg	2,400 mg or less	
Carbohydrates	21 g	250 g or more	
Protein	46 g	55 g to 90 g	

133

CHUNKY CHICKEN CHILI

Here's chili on the light side. If a big bowl o' red is one of your guilty pleasures, you'll love the gutsy flavor of this low-fat version.

▼ *Low-fat*
▽ *Low-calorie*
   Prep time: 15 minutes plus chilling
   Cooking time: 20 minutes
○ *Degree of difficulty: easy*

1 **pound boneless, skinless chicken *or* turkey breast, cut into 1-inch cubes**
1 **teaspoon vegetable oil, divided**
1 **cup minced onions**
1 **tablespoon minced garlic**
2 **teaspoons chili powder**
½ **teaspoon cumin**
⅛ **teaspoon cinnamon**
1 **can (14½ *or* 16 ounces) tomatoes, liquid reserved**
1 **can (13¾ *or* 14½ ounces) chicken broth *or* 1¾ cups Rich Chicken Stock (recipe, page 29)**
1 **can (15 ounces) pinto beans, drained and rinsed**
1 **can (15 ounces) red kidney beans, drained and rinsed**
1 **package (10 ounces) frozen succotash**

1 Pat chicken dry on paper towels. Heat ½ teaspoon of the oil in a large saucepan over high heat. Add half the chicken pieces and brown well on all sides; transfer with a slotted spoon to a plate. Repeat with remaining ½ teaspoon oil and chicken.

2 Add onions to saucepan; cover and cook over medium heat until tender, 5 minutes. Stir in garlic, chili powder, cumin, and cinnamon; cook 30 seconds. Add tomatoes with liquid; bring to a boil. Add chicken broth, beans, and succotash; bring to a boil. Reduce heat and simmer 10 minutes. Add chicken and simmer 5 minutes more. Makes 6 servings.

PER SERVING		DAILY GOAL
Calories	263	2,000 (F), 2,500 (M)
Total Fat	4 g	60 g or less (F), 70 g or less (M)
Saturated fat	0 g	20 g or less (F), 23 g or less (M)
Cholesterol	44 mg	300 mg or less
Sodium	736 mg	2,400 mg or less
Carbohydrates	30 g	250 g or more
Protein	27 g	55 g to 90 g

134

SPICED TURKEY-BLACK BEAN CHILI

Ground turkey to the rescue again in this fast chili. Make it ahead for an effortless dinner tomorrow.

▼ *Low-calorie*
Prep time: 15 minutes
Cooking time: 30 minutes
○ *Degree of difficulty: easy*

2 **tablespoons vegetable oil**
1 **onion, diced**
2 **garlic cloves, minced**
1½ **tablespoons chili powder**
2 **teaspoons cumin**
1 **bay leaf**
1 **teaspoon aniseed**
½ **teaspoon ground coriander**
8 **ounces ground turkey**
1 **can (16 ounces) whole tomatoes in puree**
1 **can (16 ounces) black beans, drained and rinsed**
1 **red pepper, diced**
1 **to 2 jalapeño peppers, seeded and minced**
¼ **teaspoon salt**

¼ **teaspoon ground red pepper**
2 **tablespoons minced fresh cilantro**
Shredded cheddar cheese, cilantro leaves, minced green onions, and tortilla chips, for garnish

1 Heat oil in a medium Dutch oven over medium-high heat. Add onion and cook, stirring, until softened, 5 minutes. Stir in garlic, chili powder, cumin, bay leaf, aniseed, and coriander. Cook, stirring constantly, 3 minutes, being careful not to burn. Stir in turkey and cook, breaking up meat with a spoon, until meat is no longer pink, 5 to 7 minutes.

2 Add tomatoes with puree, black beans, sweet pepper, jalapeño, salt, and ground red pepper; bring to a boil. Reduce heat and simmer uncovered, stirring occasionally, 30 minutes. Stir in cilantro. Spoon into bowls and serve with garnishes. Makes 4 servings.

PER SERVING		DAILY GOAL
Calories	275	2,000 (F), 2,500 (M)
Total Fat	12 g	60 g or less (F), 70 g or less (M)
Saturated fat	2 g	20 g or less (F), 23 g or less (M)
Cholesterol	41 mg	300 mg or less
Sodium	584 mg	2,400 mg or less
Carbohydrates	26 g	250 g or more
Protein	17 g	55 g to 90 g

KID-PLEASING CHILI

For all those big and little kids, here's a vat of chili that's not too spicy. To keep things lean, we've cooked this up with ground turkey, but ground chicken or beef are tasty, too.

▼ *Low-fat*
▽ *Low-calorie*
Prep time: 10 minutes
Cooking time: 1¾ hours
○ *Degree of difficulty: easy*

2 **teaspoons vegetable oil**
1 **cup chopped onions**
1 **cup chopped celery**
1½ **teaspoons minced garlic**
1 **pound ground turkey**
1 **can (28 ounces) tomatoes, cut up and liquid reserved**
1 **can (13¾ or 14½ ounces) beef *or* chicken broth *or* 1¾ cups Hearty Beef Stock (recipe, page 30) *or* Rich Chicken Stock (recipe, page 29)**
2 **to 3 teaspoons chili powder**
1 **teaspoon cumin**
¾ **teaspoon salt**

½ teaspoon oregano
¼ teaspoon freshly ground pepper
2 cans (16 ounces each) pinto, red, *or* black beans, drained and rinsed
1 cup frozen whole-kernel corn
1 tablespoon chopped fresh parsley

1 Heat oil in a large Dutch oven over high heat. Add onions, celery, and garlic; cook until vegetables are softened, 3 minutes. Add turkey and cook, stirring to break up meat with a spoon, until lightly browned, 5 minutes.

2 Add tomatoes with liquid, beef or chicken broth, chili powder, cumin, salt, oregano, and pepper; bring to a boil. Reduce heat to low; cover, and simmer 1 hour. Add beans and corn; cover and simmer 15 minutes.

3 Increase heat to medium. Uncover chili and cook, stirring, until thickened, about 15 minutes more. Stir in parsley. Makes 6 servings.

PER SERVING		DAILY GOAL
Calories	283	2,000 (F), 2,500 (M)
Total Fat	8 g	60 g or less (F), 70 g or less (M)
Saturated fat	1 g	20 g or less (F), 23 g or less (M)
Cholesterol	55 mg	300 mg or less
Sodium	1,145 mg	2,400 mg or less
Carbohydrates	30 g	250 g or more
Protein	22 g	55 g to 90 g

GREAT CHILI FIXINGS: THE BEST CHILI GO-WITHS AND COOL DOWNS

Chili loves a crowd, a mess of tasty toppers, and sides to go with it. Here are a few of our favorites:

• **Sour cream or low-fat or non-fat plain yogurt:** Serve a dollop on its own or jazzed up with few spoonfuls of chopped fresh cilantro and a pinch of cumin for a zippy topping.

• **Grated cheese:** Shredded sharp cheddar or Monterey Jack are chili favorites, but give shavings of fresh Parmesan a try.

• **Onions of all colors:** The taste and crunch of chopped fresh onions make them classic chili toppers. Use red, yellow, or green onions, or chopped shallots if the mood and chili heat are milder.

• **The cool crunch of lettuce:** The crisper, the better. Try shredded iceberg, curly endive or Romaine lettuces, or watercress.

• **A scattering of this 'n' that:** Diced tomato, avocado, sliced ripe olives, fresh cilantro leaves, fresh tortillas, and lime wedges all go with chili.

• **Home-baked tortilla chips:** Preheat oven to 450°F. Cut 4 corn tortillas into 8 wedges each. Bake on a cookie sheet 5 to 6 minutes or until crisp. Cool completely. Makes 32 chips.

• **Guacamole:** Mash 2 ripe avocados, ¼ cup minced red onion, 2 tablespoons fresh lime juice, ½ teaspoon salt, and ¼ teaspoon red pepper sauce in a medium bowl with a large fork or potato masher until blended. Makes 2 cups.

TOTALLY VEGETARIAN CHILI

The flavor of this robust, meatless chili comes from the chipotle chilies—jalapeños that have been smoked.

▼ *Low-fat*
Prep time: 30 minutes plus soaking
Cooking time: 1¾ hours
○ *Degree of difficulty: easy*

1½ **cups dried black beans**
1½ **cups dried small red beans**
2 **dried pasilla *or* ancho chilies**
 Water
2 **dried chipotle chilies *or* 1 can (7 ounces) chipotle chilies in adobo***
1 **tablespoon vegetable oil**
3 **cups chopped onions**
1 **green pepper, diced**
1 **red pepper, diced**
1 **tablespoon cumin**
1 **tablespoon minced garlic**
2 **dried de árbol* *or* serrano chilies**
1 **can (14 ounces) tomatoes, chopped and liquid reserved**
1 **large butternut squash, peeled and cut into ¾-inch dice (5 cups)**
1 **tablespoon salt**
1 **package (10 ounces) frozen lima beans**
 Plain yogurt, lime wedges, and flour tortillas

1 Rinse beans and pick over for small stones and shriveled beans. In a large bowl, cover beans with 2 inches water and soak overnight. (To quick-soak: Combine beans with water to cover by 2 inches in a large saucepan and bring to a boil; boil 2 minutes. Cover and let stand 1 hour.) Drain in a colander.

2 Remove stems and seeds from pasilla chilies and dried chipotle, if using. Heat a large cast-iron skillet over medium-low heat. Toast chilies, turning frequently, until fragrant and pliable, 2 minutes. (Be careful not to get the peppery smoke in your eyes.)

3 Transfer chilies to a blender. Bring ½ cup water to a boil; add to chilies and puree until smooth. Set aside. (For chipotles in adobo, puree in a clean blender until smooth. Reserve 2 tablespoons. Refrigerate remaining puree for another use.)

4 Heat oil in a large Dutch oven over medium-high heat. Add onions and red and green peppers; cook 10 minutes. Stir in cumin, garlic, and de árbol chilies; cook 30 seconds. Add drained beans, pasilla puree (and reserved chipotle-in-adobo puree if using), and 6½ cups water; bring to a boil, cover, and simmer until beans are almost tender, 1 hour.

5 Stir in tomatoes with liquid, squash and salt. Return to a boil. Reduce heat, cover and cook 10 minutes. Add lima beans and cook 20 minutes more. Remove de árbol chilies. Serve with a dollop of yogurt, lime wedges, and tortillas. Makes 10 servings.

*Dried and canned chilies can be ordered from Mo-Hotta Mo-Betta, 800-462-3220.

PER SERVING WITH ONE TORTILLA		DAILY GOAL
Calories	548	2,000 (F), 2,500 (M)
Total Fat	5 g	60 g or less (F), 70 g or less (M)
Saturated fat	2 g	20 g or less (F), 23 g or less (M)
Cholesterol	3 mg	300 mg or less
Sodium	1,196 mg	2,400 mg or less
Carbohydrates	105 g	250 g or more
Protein	26 g	55 g to 90 g

THREE-BEAN CHILI

With a batch of our homemade Zesty Tomato Sauce at the ready, you can spice up a batch of this vegetarian chili in minutes.

Prep time: 10 minutes
Cooking time: 15 minutes
O *Degree of difficulty: easy*

1½ teaspoons coriander
1½ teaspoons cumin
½ teaspoon chili powder
1 can (15 ounces) kidney beans, drained and rinsed
1 can (15 ounces) chick-peas (garbanzo beans), drained and rinsed
1 can (15 ounces) white beans, drained and rinsed
1 can (4 ounces) whole green chilies, cut into ½-inch pieces and liquid reserved
¼ teaspoon salt
3 cups Zesty Tomato Sauce (recipe at right) *or* prepared tomato sauce
1 cup shredded Monterey Jack cheese *or* shredded jicama

Toast coriander, cumin, and chili powder in a large saucepan over medium-high heat, stirring constantly, 3 minutes. (Be careful not to burn.) Add kidney beans, chick-peas, white beans, chilies with liquid, salt, and tomato sauce; bring to a boil. Reduce heat and simmer 10 minutes or until thickened. Spoon into bowls and top with shredded cheese. Makes 4 servings.

PER SERVING		DAILY GOAL
Calories	394	2,000 (F), 2,500 (M)
Total Fat	14 g	60 g or less (F), 70 g or less (M)
Saturated fat	6 g	20 g or less (F), 23 g or less (M)
Cholesterol	30 mg	300 mg or less
Sodium	1,462 mg	2,400 mg or less
Carbohydrates	46 g	250 g or more
Protein	23 g	55 g to 90 g

ZESTY TOMATO SAUCE

Prep time: 20 minutes
Cooking time: 1¼ hours
O *Degree of difficulty: easy*

3 medium carrots, peeled and cut into ½-inch pieces
1 celery rib, cut into 1-inch pieces

2 tablespoons olive oil
1 cup chopped onions
1 tablespoon plus 1 teaspoon minced garlic
2 tablespoons tomato paste
2 large cans (35 ounces each) Italian plum tomatoes, chopped, with their liquid (*or* 8 pounds fresh tomatoes, peeled, seeded and chopped)
3 tablespoons chopped fresh flat-leaf parsley
1½ teaspoons salt
½ teaspoon freshly ground pepper
½ teaspoon red pepper flakes

1 Pulse carrots in a food processor until chopped fine; transfer to a medium bowl. Add celery and pulse until chopped fine, then add to carrots.

2 Heat oil in a large Dutch oven over medium-high heat. Add onions and garlic and cook until onions are softened, 3 minutes. Add carrots and celery and continue cooking, stirring occasionally, 5 minutes. Stir in tomato paste and cook 2 minutes more. Add tomatoes with liquid, parsley, salt, pepper and red pepper flakes.

Bring to a boil, then reduce heat to medium-low and simmer uncovered 1 hour. Makes 8 cups with canned tomatoes, 9 cups with fresh.

PER 1 CUP		DAILY GOAL
Calories	95	2,000 (F), 2,500 (M)
Total Fat	4 g	60 g or less (F), 70 g or less (M)
Saturated fat	1 g	20 g or less (F), 23 g or less (M)
Cholesterol	0 mg	300 mg or less
Sodium	768 mg	2,400 mg or less
Carbohydrates	15 g	250 g or more
Protein	3 g	55 g to 90 g

BIG BARLEY CHILI

This is a meatless chili that's light on the fat, but one that even a die-hard Texan would love. It's best if these big and bold flavors mellow overnight.

▼ *Low-fat*
▽ *Low-calorie*
   Prep time: 10 minutes
   Cooking time: 45 minutes
○ *Degree of difficulty: easy*

3 **cups water**
1 **cup pearl barley**
1 **tablespoon vegetable oil**
2 **cups chopped onions**
1 **red *or* yellow pepper, diced**
1 **tablespoon minced garlic**
2 **tablespoons chili powder**
1 **tablespoon cumin**
¾ **teaspoon salt**
¼ **teaspoon ground red pepper**
1 **can (13¾ *or* 14½ ounces) chicken broth *or* 1¾ cups Rich Chicken Stock (recipe, page 29) plus enough water to equal 3 cups**
1 **can (14 ounces) original *or* Mexican-style stewed tomatoes**
1 **can (15 ounces) red kidney beans, drained and rinsed**
1 **can (15 ounces) black beans, drained and rinsed**
1 **cup frozen black-eyed peas Plain low-fat *or* non-fat yogurt**

1 Bring 3 cups water to a boil; add barley. Reduce heat to medium and cook until barley is just tender, 20 minutes. Drain.

2 Heat oil in a 6-quart Dutch oven over medium-high heat. Add onions and pepper; cover and cook, stirring occasionally, until vegetables are tender, 5 minutes. Stir in garlic, chili powder, cumin, salt, and red pepper and cook until fragrant, 30 seconds. Add cooked barley, chicken broth, tomatoes, kidney beans, black beans, and black-eyed peas.

3 Bring chili to a boil. Reduce heat and simmer uncovered until barley is very tender and chili is slightly thickened, 20 minutes. Serve with yogurt if desired. Makes 6 servings.

PER SERVING		DAILY GOAL
Calories	347	2,000 (F), 2,500 (M)
Total Fat	5 g	60 g or less (F), 70 g or less (M)
Saturated fat	0 g	20 g or less (F), 23 g or less (M)
Cholesterol	0 mg	300 mg or less
Sodium	965 mg	2,400 mg or less
Carbohydrates	59 g	250 g or more
Protein	16 g	55 g to 90 g

NOTES

_____
_____
_____
_____
_____
_____
_____
_____
_____
_____
_____

METRIC COOKING HINTS

By making a few conversions, cooks in Australia, Canada, and the United Kingdom can use the recipes in Ladies' Home Journal® *100 Great Soup, Stew & Chili Recipes* with confidence. The charts on this page provide a guide for converting measurements from the U.S. customary system, which is used throughout this book, to the imperial and metric systems. There also is a conversion table for oven temperatures to accommodate the differences in oven calibrations.

Volume and Weight: Americans traditionally use cup measures for liquid and solid ingredients. The chart (top right) shows the approximate imperial and metric equivalents. If you are accustomed to weighing solid ingredients, here are some helpful approximate equivalents.
■ 1 cup butter, castor sugar, or rice = 8 ounces = about 250 grams
■ 1 cup flour = 4 ounces = about 125 grams
■ 1 cup icing sugar = 5 ounces = about 150 grams
  Spoon measures are used for smaller amounts of ingredients. Although the size of the tablespoon varies slightly among countries, for practical purposes and for recipes in this book, a straight substitution is all that's necessary.
  Measurements made using cups or spoons should always be level, unless stated otherwise.

Product Differences: Most of the ingredients called for in the recipes in this book are available in English-speaking countries. However, some are known by different names. Here are some common American ingredients and their possible counterparts:
■ Sugar is granulated or castor sugar.
■ Powdered sugar is icing sugar.
■ All-purpose flour is plain household flour or white flour. When self-rising flour is used in place of all-purpose flour in a recipe that calls for leavening, omit the leavening agent (baking soda or baking powder) and salt.
■ Light corn syrup is golden syrup.
■ Cornstarch is cornflour.
■ Baking soda is bicarbonate of soda.
■ Vanilla is vanilla essence.

USEFUL EQUIVALENTS

⅛ teaspoon = 0.5 ml
¼ teaspoon = 1 ml
½ teaspoon = 2 ml
1 teaspoon = 5 ml
¼ cup = 2 fluid ounces = 50 ml
⅓ cup = 3 fluid ounces = 75 ml
½ cup = 4 fluid ounces = 125 ml
⅔ cup = 5 fluid ounces = 150 ml
¾ cup = 6 fluid ounces = 175 ml
1 cup = 8 fluid ounces = 250 ml
2 cups = 1 pint
2 pints = 1 litre
½ inch = 1 centimetre
1 inch = 2 centimetres

BAKING PAN SIZES

American	Metric
8x1½-inch round baking pan	20x4-centimetre sandwich or cake tin
9x1½-inch round baking pan	23x3.5-centimetre sandwich or cake tin
11x7x1½-inch baking pan	28x18x4-centimetre baking pan
13x9x2-inch baking pan	32.5x23x5-centimetre baking pan
2-quart rectangular baking dish	30x19x5-centimetre baking pan
15x10x2-inch baking pan	38x25.5x2.5-centimetre baking pan (Swiss roll tin)
9-inch pie plate	22x4- or 23x4-centimetre pie plate
7- or 8-inch springform pan	18- or 20-centimetre springform or loose-bottom cake tin
9x5x3-inch loaf pan	23x13x6-centimetre or 2-pound narrow loaf pan or paté tin
1½-quart casserole	1.5-litre casserole
2-quart casserole	2-litre casserole

OVEN TEMPERATURE EQUIVALENTS

Fahrenheit Setting	Celsius Setting*	Gas Setting
300°F	150°C	Gas Mark 2
325°F	160°C	Gas Mark 3
350°F	180°C	Gas Mark 4
375°F	190°C	Gas Mark 5
400°F	200°C	Gas Mark 6
425°F	220°C	Gas Mark 7
450°F	230°C	Gas Mark 8
Broil		Grill

*Electric and gas ovens may be calibrated using Celsius. However, increase the Celsius setting 10 to 20 degrees when cooking above 160°C with an electric oven. For convection or forced-air ovens (gas or electric), lower the temperature setting 10°C when cooking at all heat levels.

$AVE UP TO $7 on